One man's year long journey
through internet dating

romance - sex - discovery

discovery

romance

new friends

My First 32
Coffee
Dates

secret passions

sex

relationships

by M. Lyman Hill

Illustrations - Cartoons: Mark Hill
Editing by: Valerie Peck
and Catherine Van Herrin

dating secrets

My First 32 Coffee Dates
One man's year long journey through internet dating

By M. Lyman Hill

Dedicated to all those people looking for love online

Illustrations – Cartoons: Mark Hill
Copy Editing by: Valerie Peck
and Catherine Van Herrin

LEGAL NOTICE
Author: M. Lyman Hill
Title: My First 32 Coffee Dates

Copyright © 2011, M. Lyman Hill
Round-2 Communications Presents

Introduction

In my lifetime, I have noticed that most people I know, me included, are either in a relationship, trying to get in one, or trying to get out of one. Relationships seem to be of the utmost importance to adults. My own relationships have been a mixed bag of joy and pain, erotic and dull, connected and distant. I've also found that most of my relationships have become more difficult as time passes, and that some were even emotionally damaging to me, but still I persist. I've stayed in bad relationships and left good ones.

Maybe this kind of thing has happened to you: I'd been going along in an otherwise wonderful life with its normal, everyday ups and downs when I stopped long enough to find myself at a crossroads, accompanied by more than a few uncomfortable feelings. "Is this my life?" "Why do I feel 'stuck'? " "Is this all there is?" and the oh-so-devastating but usual, "Oh my God -- am I having a midlife crisis?" Then, "Hold on now, wait a minute -- I can't be – this is not a crisis, this is my life. Calm down; get a grip."

I am not sure how, but that day I realized I'd spent much of my life adapting myself to please others, and that was why my relationships did not work. Being "me" was the problem when it should have been the benefit. I was the genuine, bona fide "people pleaser."

Now, just for the record, I never married or even dated my secretary. I'm not attracted to younger women. Well, okay, there are a few. I don't own anything with wheels that is painted red. So, I figured, "Okay; throw out the stereotypical midlife crisis and get real with me – I just want to be me – not a stereotype."

Maybe I'm a lot more like everyone else than I think: For example, I love falling in love and hate falling out of it. I have a pretty good idea that many people can relate to that. I think everyone should fall in love many times in his or her life or at least fall in love again with the same person. You know that feeling…nothing else is important except getting to know, be with, and interact with that someone special. You doodle, can't get any work done, write silly poems and invent words (otherwise known as "pet names") for your loved one. Falling in love is not very practical or productive, but when it happens none of that seems to matter. I realized that day that if I set aside my fears, the risk of the pain and/or rejection, then I'd truly have nothing to lose, but in fact, a life experience to gain: the experience of getting to know someone and even "falling a little in love" just a little bit. I figured it this way: it's either that or shut myself off to every potential relationship until I feel like the one that's *really* worth it comes along. But how do I know how much something is worth unless I try?

I'll be upfront about something else: I can't tell this story well without fictionalizing it a little bit. So, get ready: this is the man's perspective on *Sex in the City*. The events that I have turned into a kind of fiction help me describe real-life events without interrupting or exposing the lives of the women I met.

But I really did it; I met 32 women for coffee and dated many of them after coffee. I went through thousands of online ads, met women around the world, dated them and had some interesting, sexy and crazy experiences I want to share. What I saw, thought, felt and did during my one-year foray through the online dating machine is pretty good food for thought; for both men and women out there in the same boat.

This book is not an exposé; these are real people who I spent time with and care about, so names, dates, places, certain events and particular situations have been changed to protect these ladies' identities.

I also think everyone is interested in others' romantic experiences because this is how they get to compare it to their own. It is a little voyeuristic, sure, but it somehow helps us.

When I started writing this book, I had met two very special women with whom I had enjoyed longer-term relationships. One I am with today, who is helping me edit these lines and words; and the other I dated for eighteen months and still keep in touch with. My goal, above all things, is not to lose any real connections I made, or lose the wonder and beauty of friendship. Women are unique, weird, lovable and just plain fun. And my connection to them is precious to me.

Afterthoughts: *"It seems to me that we bring into a relationship everything we need in order for it to be successful, and also that perhaps it is not the nature of relationships to last forever."*

"A woman once said to me that what women want is to be someone's priority. I thought about this for a long time and decided that is like settling for as little as you can get and scaring the hell out of the guy in the process."

Chapter One

The adventure begins

Imagine looking over tens of thousands of personal ads in order to exchange thousands of emails, to get to hundreds of phone calls, to then set 32 coffee dates. Because I work professionally in the Internet technology industry, using online dating and matching services came very easily to me – or, at least it was natural, but it was also exhausting. I am the kind of man who is driven. You know – Mr. Type A+. So, when my marriage failed, I moved into an apartment I found myself looking for love again online. I'm just not one to waste time.

Imagine meeting 32 very different women for coffee in less than nine months, then dating a few of them: nurses, psychologists, attorneys, school teachers, a couple of legal secretaries, a surf shop owner, a veterinarian, a flight attendant, a model, several real estate agents, and on and on. Some were nice and some were very nice, but off in a world of their own. Imagine that, and you'll be right there with me because that is what I went through in just one year's time.

December in the San Francisco Bay area is a great time – the sky is clear, the temperatures are cool, and the days are short -- which leaves long nights. I was starting a new job with a large consulting company as an engagement manager, getting back into running again and other new ways to improve my body, mind and spirit. I needed to keep my mind busy. Pretty soon, after acclimating myself to this new job and my new lifestyle, I was on a roll. I had established my preferred "pace."

I became very involved in my work, which I do happen to enjoy, thankfully, and soon found myself working 12-hour days. Sure, I liked the work, but it was just that: work. Not exactly what I envisioned for my life, post-divorce. Between my job, life's little chores, running and hiking and Internet dating, most of my time was gone. And then, of course, I had to sleep.

I kept taking on more responsibility at work until I felt I was going to burst; running hard every morning helped me battle the stress. I'd run early in the morning, around 4 a.m. Then I'd make the train ride into the city, during which time I'd use a wireless connection to send and reply to emails to keep up with my growing number of connections.

One thing that happens after starting over is that you find you have quite a lot of time on your hands -- time you did not realize you had, even when you were working like a madman and in a relationship.

For years, maybe even decades, I'd tried to "fit into" my relationships. It was akin to casting a new mold, a new shape for me for each relationship. At the time, I suppose I thought women expected it of me. However, the truth was, I was the only one expecting it of me. Why was I the one who always had to change or otherwise alter my personality, looks, etc., for the other person? After thinking about that for a while, I realize what a waste of time this was and declared myself "done with that!" I was done with trying to "fit" into another person's lifestyle, and I made a vow that "never again" would I compromise myself and my personality or principles to get into a relationship.

I am a really nice man with a great deal to offer a woman. "Nice men finish last," as the old adage goes, right? I often realized this was true. Nice men *do* often sacrifice themselves for others because self-sacrifice seems like a virtue. And unfortunately, it is in my nature to do that. But I began to embrace a part of myself, a part of me that I appreciated and liked, but that I had overlooked in my younger years, and I vowed never to overlook again -- the essence of who I am and all those things I loved but had sacrificed over the years for the sake of the other person in the relationship.

I also formed a definition of a "good relationship" in my mind: the kind where I could just be myself and be comfortable, knowing that the woman I was with actually benefited from me being me. I was determined to get out there and really enjoy life again.

I am a Renaissance guy, but not the stereotype, and despite rumors to the contrary, I don't have much of an ego. Nope, I am the kind of guy who gets off on helping other people be successful. That's why I have been successful in my life and career. My goal for a relationship was similarly clear: find the best relationship "fit" for both parties; one in which I can be myself and she can be herself, and we both would be a benefit to each other just by being "us." Kinda poetic, huh?

I thought about relationships and my approach to them for a long time. I realized after all that thinking that I was different now than when I was younger. As a young man, I was very pliable, not fully formed -- so when I met a woman, we went off to design a life together which helped form both of us. When I took stock of my approach to relationships again, as the older, "newer me," I found it next to impossible to merge my life with anyone because, after all, it was "my life" I was dealing with here – I had made some great inroads into it, appreciated it, and I wasn't as malleable or willing to let go of the things I had done and learned that meant a lot to me. So, the only alternatives were to find a woman who was flexible or a woman who was like me. Or both.

I love the outdoors and ballet; I attend local theater and play rock and roll real loud; I eat pizza and French food; I'm comfortable dining at small-plate venues and roadside stands, drinking fine wine and ginger ale, and looking at fine art and sports. In fact, my interests are so varied that I never get "bored" or stale I figured that a woman who would be the best match for me would be someone who enjoyed a variety of things, as well. Of course that was not who I was attracting, nor had attracted in the past.

When I moved from the condo I shared with my ex-wife to a two-bedroom Fremont apartment, I took only a few essentials: me, my computer, my clothes, one of our three TVs and my keepsakes. I bought a desk, a bed and some things to cook with. One of the advantages of Spartan living is that there is very little housework required. So, factoring in very little housework, long nights and living alone meant that I had some time on my hands – more time, in fact, than I needed and felt was healthy for me.

Of course I thought about waiting; the best advice after a breakup is to wait until sometime passes to get beyond the broken relationship and then see how things go; at least that is what I heard from several well-meaning people. I hope you'll understand that I was completely ready to disconnect from my ex when I did. My marriage went south just one year into it, and four years later, we were virtual roommates – I lived in my part of the condo and she in hers. Conversation was kept to a minimum and sex had stopped. She was the only woman I had ever known to personify the true "couch potato."

Still, all those concerned about me insisted that I "wait a little while." So, as a safeguard, I decided to just test the waters -- you know, put my toes in and see how warm the water was.

Let me further explain a little more about the kind of person I am: where I shine, you'd better get sunglasses, and where I am dull I am dumb as a post. The one person I *do* know very well is me – I know that when I start something in which I am really interested, a wildfire of activity will follow. I am the single most productive person I have ever met when I am interested – modest, too. So after 10 seconds of testing the water I not only jumped in but splashed around pretty aggressively two to four hours a day.

All right, I did it, I jumped in, I had the time, had the will, and I did it. Now I was wet from jumping in and did not know where to swim next. Because I am a project manager, I did what came naturally to me – I made a plan. Because the pool was so big, I needed a way to get to just the right woman through tens of thousands of prospects on 100 websites.

Afterthoughts: *"Contrary to popular culture, there are many women who think about sex all the time. I met them"*

GREAT EXPECTATIONS

"The biggest disappointment I had while dating was to get worked up by email and telephone, only to be let down when we met for coffee." "I never felt I was wasting my time meeting so many women, because though I was looking for a soul mate, everyone I met was so interesting."

Chapter Two

Fact vs. Fiction

The first thing I noticed when looking online was that there were a LOT of ads! I got the impression that millions of women were looking for love. Imagine that – at any moment, millions of people are looking for love – that's pretty cool, but it's kind of daunting, too. That was really something to think about. How do we average souls find love in such an ocean of people? "Millions" being a bit of an exaggeration still made me think that online dating had improved greatly from the bulletin board and newspaper ad days in the past, when maybe, by some chance, someone found your ad. Yet here were these sophisticated websites whose creators and administrators understood at least some aspects of relationship dynamics and therefore brought in these millions of would-be daters from around the globe.

Just for the fun of it and without registering, I started looking at ads (profiles) of women from all around the world. My experience told me that many of the ads and photos were not very good at describing who I would find if I actually met many of the women I was reading about. Some of the photos were staged glamour shots, and for sure every one of these women were looking their best. After all, who would post a picture of themselves just getting out of bed or describe themselves as "sleep late, can't function until I have my coffee, love to watch TV – reality shows are my life"? Nope, they might post a funny photo of themselves and say something like, "I'm laid back, sleep late on Sundays, love to cook, and enjoy gardening."

It's interesting that people seem to naturally see themselves in a better light then they actually are – me included – so when I understood that, I began developing a science of understanding the lingo and symbols women use in their ads. (Remember, I'm an Internet project manager and an engineer. I can't help it.)

Some of the photos were for show, such as standing on a mountain, walking along the beach or dressed for dinner – now, these were helpful if the ad had some detail to match them to the photo – cool! But, for example, one woman posted 20 photos, which certainly made it easier for me to tell a lot more about her, but there was the age-old question: When were the photos taken?

Sure, there were great photos of women sailing, women on motorbikes, horseback riding, diving, pictures of their cats, grouped with friends (I assumed), posing with their exes, and on and on. Photos were helpful in a way, in that they posed curious questions and otherwise made the experience of voyeurism better.

The second challenge was understanding monikers, handles, nicknames, emoticons, banner ads and headlines. "Come fly with me!" Susan94111 might mean she lives in San Francisco and is a pilot; or it might mean she couldn't think of anything clever to say. "Catch me if you can" – redrunnergirl3 might mean she is a runner and has red hair, or it might mean she wears red as her killer outfit and loves running around the couch, if you get the drift. It is at that moment of revelation when I discovered that if I was going to get serious about this, I needed a tagline too, and some kind of moniker that would describe me to the tee: "Looking for someone different?" "Coffee and Conversation" -- brilliant; I would become coffee_and_conversation – or something like that.

The third challenge facing me as a would-be online dater was that many women don't write well. Most of the ads say so little about the person and what they like to do or who they are that it's just not worth writing them to find out. I figured if a woman couldn't put together a pretty good overall picture of herself in words at the outset, she probably wouldn't be able to do so in a return email. This kind of hype was like a sales pitch for passersby.

Later, I discovered that some of the sites offer paid writers to spiff up the ads for the poor writers. Okay, now, but it is supposed to be that way? These women want to find the best man they can, so why not fish with the best bait – right? While I can certainly see where that makes sense to them, what about the hapless, hopeless romantics out there (that would be me) who think, "Wow, she's terrific-looking AND she can write!"

This presented me with yet another challenge: I realized I had to look very objectively at the each ad and decipher who that person really is – I knew that, in order to not be fooled, I was going to have to do a lot of reading and re-reading between the lines.

Then there is the basic human desire to represent one's self in the best light – you know, dressed well when we mostly live in running pants and a T-shirt. That left me with the chore of figuring out how much that was written in an ad was accurate, projected, exaggerated or just plain fiction.

Take the case of the Dominatrix trolling for her next victim: "I am a strong independent woman, natural leader, I have my kinks, and I want it all."

Then here's the single mom looking for hubby number three: "I am a strong independent woman, eclectic, full of life, love family."

The serial dater who has no interest in relationships writes: "Strong, independent, wild, walks on the beach, full of life, let's go for it." Enough said? So, which is better, "hot redhead vixen," or "cool purrrfict kitten?" It is very difficult to get a good image of the person on the other end just from these kinds of ads. I knew I really had to work at it.

I needed some science that was obvious; otherwise, I would drown in the details of trying to figure out these women from their profiles. The science I developed was matching photos, rhetoric and personality descriptions to body types, career choices and family, and to ask specific follow-up questions. I could ask anything in private messages. One example was a wonderful redhead who had posted photos of her hiking, dressed up for the symphony, and in her business garb. Not too many photos, true, but enough to get the idea that she had a wide range of interests. Her profile stated that she liked the arts and nature, and in her bio, I read that she spent lots of time hiking in the hills behind her house. So, I emailed her and asked how many time she hikes a month. Her answer was, "One or two." From that, I could see she was projecting her desire to hike a lot more than she did, and likely had other anomalies in her profile that I might have to weed through.

The online world presents biographical information – such as age, height, hair and eye color, profession, income, weight or frame, photos, and some form of a filtering system – the "likes and dislikes" section, in which a potential dater indicates what they are interested in or where they stand politically and what they might have in common with their prospective suitors. All have some type of written profile. Sometimes a site has a personality test to compare and match you to another, along with ways to engage the would-be dater, such as surveys; and the all-important "feedback system" with which to communicate with potential dates (for a fee).

First, the photos provided immediate interest for me, being the visual person I am – no photos, no interest -- well, sort of. Again, the filtering systems offered by these dating sites often were lists of what the women were interested in, such as music, movies and travel. The written profiles came in all shapes; some were elaborate and well-written, but most were very short – just a few lines. The ones IN ALL CAPS I just ignored.

On one site, I took advantage of the "Kiss-ability" survey and scored well – I just smiled and moved on. Then, there was the feedback system, which no site of any kind allowed you to use unless you registered. You could look but not touch until you paid the money.

Then there were the contacts from would-be daters addressed to me without photos when I had specifically asked for them. Okay, I am not a rock of discipline; I was open to all, but all I had time for, that is.

Afterthoughts: *"It is a waste of time to think everyone will want to learn what words mean to me, so I gave up on that and made a lot more friends by learning their language and then sharing mine."*

10 YEARS OLD PHOTOS

Chapter Three

Regression and couches

I actually had tried this online dating thing before, back in the early days of the Internet. It was difficult then, too, but I had some success. I "virtually met" many women, dated a few and actually married one of them.

Now, that backdrop colored all my thinking and decisions about looking for another relationship online. It was like my first love and this very day many years later had merged together -- I was faced with the age-old dilemma of whether to take the risk again to have a close relationship or just date and have fun.

I am a kid at heart; my mind is "way out there." I was in the body of a 46-year-old who acted 13 going on 30. Age 13 was my coming-out year. I was a wild child in a wild time. Everyone knows that 1971 was a turbulent year, and it was that year when I started an alternative school program for kids who otherwise refused to fit in. Junior High lasted all of 12 weeks for me – then I decided I did not need school any more. This was a time before personal computers, cell phones, fax machines and CDs, and entertainment in 1969 meant getting a guitar, some pot and friends and head over to the hot springs or the ditch behind the school or anywhere there was freedom from adult supervision.

By this time I was a ward of the state, having successfully run away from home several times. The state-run boy's home I lived in hooked me up with a special program called "Opportunity Center" (OC). Special programs were rare in 1971; no one knew just what to do with all the wild children who came from the hippie movement.

I still remember opening the door of the OC for the first time. I walked down the steps with my "guardian" into the basement of the old public service building in the biggest city near the very small town I grew up in. The basement was one of those with few windows and lots of tile; that yellowed tile could also be found in the Safeway, juvenile hall and science class. The office was a half-wall just after the landing. Inside the half-wall was an old desk, a dim lamp, a rigid wooden chair, a bench and some papers plastered to the walls with tape; tape, because the wall was concrete - not very inviting…icky.

Small towns present several serious issues in getting relationships going, but somehow boys and girls always seem to find each other, and Fir Grove, Oregon, was no exception.

Fir Grove was, in 1971, the remains of a town with a grocer, gas station, trailer park and a broken-own motel which had a housing tract built behind it that my parents moved into in 1964. The "big city nearby" was Eugene, Oregon. The city and county had a population of around 120,000, all told. As the pools of candidates went, it must have been better than average because there were lots of girls looking for guys – and most of these girls found me. In fact, we seemed to find each other all the time.

 The OC was that quintessential hippie day school for kids with long hair who did not want to do school the old-fashioned way. Beside the décor, I liked it right off because the very first thing I saw after the icky half-walled office was two girls smiling at me. I was tall and lanky; even at 13 I had a mustache and beautiful long blond locks – my mother said I looked like Jesus.

The girls were very distracting to me as the principal interviewed me inside the half-wall at the beckoning of my court-appointed guardian, who was doing some paperwork and turned to me and said, "Pay attention." I was, I thought, as I looked over at the girls.

Getting laid is not exactly the driving force of young men; nope, we don't put it in those words exactly. The driving force is something under our conscious level – something without a name; a force that moves without being recognized; and those girls were smiling at me – ummmm. Yes, I was paying attention.

After the interview, my counselor left me there for my first full day of school. I thought I'd hit the jackpot. Both girls gave me a "tour." One of them turned out to be the daughter of my third-grade school teacher, and the other I had never met before. Jayne took my arm and Betty walked with us as we toured the four-room school. They had my full attention.

As my luck would have it, these two girls had made a plan to see how many guys they could seduce. So, they would greet the guys and take turns with the seduction part and keep score. After the tour the one I did not know, Betty, took me into the recreation/smoking lounge and proceeded to seduce me. We were behind the couch and she had loosened her clothes for best effect. After turning off the light she climbed on top of me. Just before we really got going, the light came on and in popped the principal, who quickly moved the couch and stopped what would have been my first time. Do you want to hear something funny? I went to Betty's wedding not 18 months later. The other girl ran away and I never saw her again.

This is how relationships happened when I was young; they just happened. The world was changing quickly, and there was a freedom about sex and relationships. You found who you could and made some connection if you wanted to. It was a time when you could meet tens or hundreds of partners – no problem -- nothing like the Internet, where millions awaited me. No interview, no coffee dates, just availability and the laws of attraction.

Take Wendy Blankenship, for example. She was a real hottie at OC. I spent many an hour building up my nerve to be bold enough to approach her, and when I finally did, we ended up spending several afternoons lying in the field south of the school in the tall grass just talking and kissing, at least until she told me she had a guy, a garbage man. This is the trouble with meeting people in life; I'd work up a head of steam and connect to these girls – but sometimes it would work and sometimes not.

So In many ways, the dating world then was completely different than it is now, and in many ways, it just goes to show you – it's still the same. It's probably never been fair, equitable or easy, even since the beginning of time. But, we keep at it, using all the tools we have at the time to fall in love.

POWER CHAT

Chapter Four

Where, oh, where to start
(or) Starting over again

My next move was clear: Which website would be right for me to find the love of my life, join it and post a profile? I found a list of 120 websites offering online personals. (This is just where I stopped counting.) There were big websites that spent a lot of money on advertising, making them easy to find; and then there were the smaller sites, specializing in niche and community dating. There were traditional, classified-type sites and specialized ones that targeted certain user groups, such as seniors, vegetarians, Catholics, gays, celibates, even truckers. (How many women truckers are there? I wonder how effective that group is.) There were highly specialized "adult" sites and religious sites.

So, where to test the waters? I spent a great deal of time reading hundreds – no, likely thousands -- of ads. I must have looked pretty comical, sitting at my desk day after day, looking at women's photos and reading about them – what a hoot. It was such a "virtual/voyeuristic" experience. Women from all over the world posting ads that I could look at – I mean, man, how cool is that? Oh, sorry – I forgot I said I didn't have an ego. Right.

There is a kinky dark side to online dating that I discovered, as well. Hey, you don't have to look for this stuff, so don't get the wrong idea here – it's listed with all of the other sites, and if you're searching, you'll come across them: Horny housewives looking to make a connection; casual sex sites; bondage sites; sexual slavery, or so-called dominance and submission sites;

regular, old-fashioned prostitution sites; massage services; bestiality sites; "millionaire" sites, and marrieds-with-benefits sites.

I spent copious hours looking into most of these; I have to admit, this stuff just fascinated me. Who are these people? Where do they live and work? How do they live? What do they tell their children when they go on a date? "Pizza's in the oven, kid, I have a sex slave waiting for me, so don't wait up?" or "Honey, I have a horny housewife to meet; please remember to pick up my dry cleaning?" The world I lived in seemed such a small place compared to the variety of experiences that other people apparently went through.

Well, I thought, I am not looking for casual sex. I am not gay. I am not Jewish (well, okay, maybe in my heart). I'm not looking for a speed date, dinner for six, not really interested in Russian women from Russia (what would we talk about and how)? I have no interest in being hand-cuffed. I do not want to import a wife from China (though they were adorable). I am not yet a senior citizen, not a hot young single, not a Texan, and not interested in a personal assistant to help me find the executive millionaire woman of my dreams, so that limited the pool of websites for me to choose from -- about 40 or so. Progress, at last!

Next, as was according to plan, I left behind all that provocative reading the Internet is so good at providing and began to imagine just what I wanted women to see in my ad. I reasoned that there were many different approaches, and that one might work well on one site and a different one on another, so the ad, photos, specification and headline should be customized to each appropriate audience. I began to feel like I was starting my career over again, rewriting each cover letter to fit the needs of the company to which I was applying. This was pretty mentally-stimulating material I found myself getting into.

Afterthought: *"A wise man said to me that to be successful at anything, you need more than that one thing to shoot for; he reasoned that it was like a fire with many branding irons in it and you take out the one that is the hottest."*

Chapter Five

Young men and getting laid

As I contemplated how my Internet profile should read and how it should look and all the many intricacies involved in posting ads to several sites, I began to feel overwhelmed and took some time away from this project to daydream again about what dating used to be like, thinking that maybe, I'd get a better feel for what I really wanted.

As I said before, the OC offered me close access to many nice girls who were very open to relationships. I had never slept with anyone I could remember (well, there was that night I got toasted and could not remember, so I'm not altogether sure), but meeting Connie, Wendy and Nedra was a refreshing experience.

These three girls were all looking for a guy, and we spent time exploring each other in detail. I loved this school! The girls were so friendly, nothing like James Madison, where you had to jump through hoops just to not get caught smoking pot.

Finally, I met Charlene. Charlene was 5' 4", well-developed and a bit of a tomboy. Her shoulder-length hair was unkempt. Most of the students at OC were from poor families and Charlene was no exception. She and her sister both attended OC. Everyone called her Chuck. I guess it was the tomboy thing.

Chuck and I hit it off right away, so my friendships with the other three girls faded fast. A self-professed virgin, Chuck was very interested in putting that behind her – and fast. A friend of mine from school (how quickly we make friends when we are young)! and I and Chuck and another girl went to Nedra's house after school. That was the day of first contact. Mars met Venus, and I wanted more and more and more. I became sexually aware at age 11; in 1969 in Eugene, Oregon, that was pretty near "normal." There was sex and drugs and rock 'n' roll. When I burst on the scene at that magical age of 13, I was getting laid very often. Charlene was one of many girls I had made out with; there had been dozens by then. All of them wanted me to touch them, and I was happy to help make that happen. I could not help but think that is why this school existed -- for my personal pleasure.

My experience thus far in my otherwise short life was that almost every girl I made friends with also wanted close intimate contact, and some wanted sex. Maybe not intercourse, but sex nonetheless.

There was one neighborhood girl who came to my bedroom at Mom's house when I was 11, and kept lying backwards on the bed, signaling me to kiss her; I was too naive to get it at the time. When I was 10, my babysitter enjoyed playing "fish out the checker from my blouse" and also liked to change her clothes while I watched. That is how it all started; some clock, some alarm, went off in my body, and I became aware of the flirtations of girls experimenting with their own sexuality right there in front of my eyes.

Now, at 46, I had to talk directly about sex with potential partners again, but this time I needed to because of "risk factors," something that didn't really exist, at least in my mind, from age 10 to 13. But in this day and time, I didn't want a 'gift' that keeps on giving. Back in 1971, we never talked about STDs; we just experimented, led by the girls who were interested. In hindsight, I must have been safe and attractive to those girls because touching, kissing and sex sure happened a lot to me.

Charlene and I did it again and again with no thought of the consequences. The field, the barn, a wayside park, a bench, the sandy shore of the river, her bedroom and mine were all wonderful places to do it – again and again. One weekend we took off for the coast with a friend of mine and did it all night in a motel he rented for us. Despite all the sex, I was losing interest in Chuck, so we broke up. A week later she came to me and said she was pregnant (I was then 13 going on 108). I was stunned; I did not know what to do, but knew for sure that I did not want to be with her and I was *certainly* not ready to be a dad.

Chuck told me some weeks later that she had lost the baby. Wow that was a lot to handle when you're 13, so I started wondering if there ever was a baby, or whether this was just a way to "keep me." Learning about sex and trust the hard (yet ever-so-free) way is a wild experience. That year I learned about manipulation, too – of the cruelest kind.

Afterthoughts: *"Unlike the typical stereotype of men and boys, I don't go around thinking about sex all the time. But I am driven to couple up"*

"I think about women much of the time; how they look, how they act and why they affect me so. Sex is there too, but not like a dog in heat!"

A BOY'S EDUCATION

Chapter Six

Toes in, head first

I officially re-ignited my online romance adventure in December 2004. Online dating then was much better than what I had experienced six years earlier, when I had just tried it once. As aforementioned, that previous experience led to a one-year long-distance romance and a brief yet stressful marriage of four years. Six years doesn't seem like a long time, but I felt like I'd been "gone" an eternity – in Internet dating terms. Yet it was just six years later that I thought it would be best to look for a woman who was the exact opposite from my ex – again, a kind of an experiment in getting more of what I wanted – but, boy, was I wrong in that strategy.

With my advanced knowledge and learned-from mistakes behind me, I made a new approach – "I will create an ad and continually refine it until I find who I am looking for and who is looking for me." But where, and for whom? I decided that this would be an organic, learning experience and a process by which I could make mistakes and correct myself as I went along to make things better. Wow, I had a grown-up moment – go figure!

Still, there were certain tactics: Fishing in a large body of water takes special equipment. To catch a big-game fish, you need strong tackle and a stiff rod and reel -- plus some patience. Okay, I admit it - that was metaphor -- maybe a meta5, in fact. The basic idea is that if you want someone better than you had before, you need the right tools and a plan. I needed to be better, too. A clear understanding of what women want would be helpful, but because women are all different, a basic understanding would just have to do.

When I was young it seemed like women were much more interested in building a family, having children and otherwise "nesting." Then, after a time, it seemed like they did not need men anymore, so almost every woman got divorced and kept their kids. Some of us men tried again; some several times. The lessons I learned from many years of relationships were that there are some things that you can just glide through with no logic and no plan – just have fun falling in and out of love over and over again. And, on the other side of the coin, of course, there are some relationships that require more logic, strategy, focus and work.

Either way you go about it, though, matters of the heart, once the heart truly takes over, is just out of your control. A relationship begins to take on a life of its own. No amount of logic will help you, and you can't argue your way through it, either. No one's listening, the least of which, your heart.

The other lesson I learned is that of course all relationships end in one way or another, and being able to deal with that is a good thing for all concerned.

Now that I am a more refined man, a better fisherman, with a basic understanding of the other half of humankind, I hoped to be more successful at keeping a relationship vital. Okay, maybe that is not the point, maybe relationships were not made to last; but I hoped they were; I hoped there were soul mates. My hopes kept me innocent and moving forward in this maze of complexity with a childlike faith that my dreams would come true.

CAREFULLY TESTING THE WATERS

Afterthoughts: *"I think people are doomed to repeat their missteps when they don't analyze what they did that caused the problem. That is why so many people meet the same kind of people over and over again."*

Chapter Seven

First loves

My first love was one of those women (girls) who could light up a room with her smile. She was blond as blond could be and had an innocence I have never known since. She was not my first girlfriend, but she was my first love. We met in juvenile hall after we had both run away from our respective homes. She was working in food services at the school, so I volunteered. We met, got along, and I want to her house after we were both out.

I set up a shrine in my closet at the boy's home I was living in and made an incantation to get her; little did I know she hardly remembered me. Alert! Sweaty palms, stutter, dry mouth, oh my. All the voices from failed attempts and ugly endings began to scream at me and I became afraid – literally afraid of what would face me if I put myself out there again. If I put myself out there, I risked rejection, loss and failure. But I was determined and went over to the coffee house where she worked. When she saw me, we smiled at each other. I guess you could say this is where coffee dates started for me.

And here I am, many years later, feeling like that same boy, hoping to catch a girl. Should I hunker down, take cover? Should I declare myself, my personality, warts and all, openly and abundantly?

My life was very comfortable. Yet I knew I had to take a risk and just dive in. If I didn't, I knew I would miss the chance of a lifetime to find my soul mate. Besides, this new Internet dating setup was a paradise -- a pool for the big kids, an extraordinary opportunity.

Risk is a funny thing. After years of being in the tech industry, I had learned that criticism was my friend and that surrounding myself with very smart people was the key to success. Smart people love to criticize, whereas weakness is risky. There is this part of me that wants to work in an ivory tower somewhere, where I cannot be hurt, never be disappointed and not meet with "Miss Disapproval." Yet to gain some semblance of greatness, it's up to me to change my ideas about failure and risk.

Transparency is the greatest way to get criticism, did you know that? Just tell someone your weaknesses or strengths, and sure enough, some teasing followed by gossip will occur until everyone knows and talks about your weaknesses or strengths. Yet allowing yourself to be "transparent" is the very characteristic that others look to when they need to trust someone. Trust is the key to all things great.

Were you to ask someone who has known me for a long time, they would say I am quite a different person from my various, previous incarnations. I've changed in so many ways. Haven't we all?

I was just 15 when I met my first love. Fifteen is that ripe old age when I also discovered I knew everything and could control anyone or any situation – it's quite frightening now to think back on. It is also sad to think of how much better I could have treated that first love -- as I would have treated her as the man I am today. But a 15-year-old just doesn't have the tools to deal with true love the way a 46-year-old may, so I cut myself some slack.

So why, at age 46, couldn't I keep a relationship going? I did it first for 15 years; then again for five years, then 18 months, three months, three hours or three minutes. I've acknowledged here that perhaps relationships are just not meant to last. But the 15-year-old in me hoped that was not true. That 15-year-old was still looking for a soul mate, the love of my life, and I'd need to look hard, because I began to realize that relationships for me were temporary for a reason: I attracted the wrong kind of woman for my lifestyle and personality – I needed someone like me, and that is one rare bird.

All right, I can hear the moaning. Some will say everyone is unique, others will proclaim that there is a 'lid for every pot,' and that is true in many ways. I actually appreciate the great diversity among us all. I'd bet most everyone feels a bit odd, alone and disconnected from time to time. You'll have to admit that some people are just odd; odd in good ways, like the runner who is faster is odd, or the scientist who is smarter is odd. Imagine what Steven King must be and feel like, or Don King, or Mick Jagger?

I am odd in that way, as well – a loner on a planet of my own, visiting earth as often as needed to make life happen -- endearingly odd.

I found that many women are attracted to the "man's-man" type -- strong, confident, good-looking and tall. Some may dispute this, but many women who like strong men are not the strong, independent types themselves. The truth is, the type of woman I was looking for was hard to find because she was out there being strong and independent, living her life.

My previous relationship took a step in that direction, the exact opposite of one before it; but my rebellion was costly because I failed to recognize that just because a woman is aggressive does not mean she is strong, and just because she is active while dating does not mean she will be so after we seal the deal. So, I married a mouth who lived on the couch.

SERIAL COFFEE DATERS

Chapter Eight

ChristianMingle.com – three months of weirdness

A friend of mine recommended a website to me based on our mutual faith. I was very skeptical, as my experience with Christian singles had been, shall we say, "not so positive." Christian singles groups have what I would call "professional singles"; men and women who, for lack of any meaningful relationship, remain single and never, ever commit. Since I was looking for a relationship, I figured this would never work. Wrong!

So I signed up and found that men pay and women could join free – what a jip! What happened to the enlightened society, equal rights, feminists, affirmative action? Okay, I admit it: it is a good idea to have women join for free, because that meant there would be more of them.

I created the best ad I could think of but quickly learned there wouldn't be much if any interaction without a photo or three. Next, I learned that what attracted me would also attract the ladies, and the opportunity to find that common ground was not going to be free.

The cost of the subscription was several hundred dollars, and the camera I bought was $600 or so. At that moment I'd wished I'd designed one of these sites. I was a web design engineer, after all – maybe I blew it right there for not creating my own dating site. But I sucked it up – I paid the fee for three months and the following Saturday morning went to my local Best Buy for a digital camera.

There were 30 cameras to choose from. I had no idea which one to pick, so I chose an expensive one that happened to be on sale and moved to the help counter. The Best Buy assistant – a young woman -- asked me what I would be doing with it, and I explained that I needed to take some photos to add to my online dating profile – she blushed and said, "This one will be perfect," while I smiled my best rakish smile at her.

Back at home, I attempted to take several shots of myself which all came out badly because I was the one holding the camera. I tried shooting myself in the mirror by putting the camera on a stick, but then I could not reach the button. Finally I put it on the bar counter and leaned down for that original orangutan look. One made me look like a psychopath, another like I was a blowfish holding the camera. I needed an impromptu studio, a place to create the kind of photos a real photographer could do. I stacked four banker's boxes holding my tax receipts on top of each other and spent several hours learning all the camera's features. Once I learned the delay and flash settings and had experimented enough to feel competent, I needed to get dressed in some charming clothes. A T-shirt and my running pants just weren't the ticket. I would need better bait for fishing.

Looking through my closet is a bit like looking at a puzzle yet unsolved. I sat there on my bed just staring at it. I owned business clothes, running clothes and outdoor clothes, but nothing in between. So I dressed in a T-shirt and a sports jacket, not really "my look," but effective enough. So I started snapping photos and editing them. After shooting 20 or so, I cropped a few and loaded them to the website – elapsed time, five hours – dollars spent, $650.

Most dating websites won't release your ad without looking it over, and they definitely won't show your images until they have been screened. That was the case with ChristianMingle.com. It took a full 40 hours to get approved. (I know, because I kept checking.) Within 10 minutes of approval, I was chatting with several women who were something like the official greeters of ChristianMingle.com. Well, maybe not official, but they were certainly eager to make my acquaintance.

Next, I had the chance to get what ChristianMingle.com calls getting "blasted." The website has an announcement service for new members to get "blasted out" to everyone looking for newbies like me. That caused a flurry of activity, which was encouraging. Emails arrived from around the country, mostly just welcoming me. Some people asked questions. The bolder ones asked me to look over their profiles.

I surfed the profiles in between chatting with the greeters and then sent off messages to some of the women I was interested in. I then took a closer look at my ad and thought of ways to improve it, so I modified it. Sadly I found that each change caused another delay of 24 to 48 hours before the ad would be approved. Similarly, when loading new photos, they would need to be approved before I could share them. This delay really discouraged me because I could not take aggressive action. I was ready to meet the woman of my dreams here!

The ads that caught my attention were those that featured nice, everyday photos. I admit the glamour photos caught my eye as well, but in a strange way they intimidated me – they made me feel as if they were out of my league. I thought that was pretty shallow thinking on my part and just let it go. But I soon found I was not as immediately interested in the content of a profile as much as the photos. I also learned that to be solely lured in by photos was a mistake, as some of what was said in the profiles provides a pretty realistic tip about who, exactly, is behind the photo.

The big trouble with ChristiannMingle.com was that there is almost no one in my area at that time. The bigger problem was that photos are not a good way to gauge how someone *really* looks. The plain truth is that no one puts their worst photos online, and thus their photos represent their best moments. This is me skiing, this is me in Cancun, and this is me 10 years ago. Look at me and my wonderful life!

After several days of emailing and some provocative chats (blush, blush), I was telephoning women in Florida, Colorado and Ohio. Not exactly California, but it was interesting. Women come in great and endless varieties, and I get it that everyone is different, but for the sake of organization I needed to categorize my contacts in some logical manner for my own purposes.

Christian woman, I reasoned, fell into three camps: the "destined" camp, where we were "destined" to date because "it must be so"; the "God tells me what to do" camp, where "God talks to me and I do what he says"; and the moderate camp, which I just label "undefined." I did not realize just how often God told women that people were meant for each other. He sure wasn't telling me.

I phoned a woman in Florida. She said, "Michael, it is so good to meet you finally." I smiled as if she could see and replied, "Lillian, I really loved your emails. I am encouraged about your love for music ministry." "Michael, I have been praying and I think God is telling me we should be going for it. He spoke to me all last night, and I feel you should come out here and we should marry."

Silence from Michael. Finally, I had to say something, and not "Sure, I'll just quit my job and be right over." I took a deep breath and said, "I think we are quite different people, Lillian, and you may have jumped the gun a bit; let's talk about this again sometime. "

Without a moment's pause she shot back, "Michael, don't you want to follow God's will?" I said, "Yes, when it is clear to me." I then asked, somewhat cleverly, I thought, "Lillian, don't you think God would speak to me, being a man who would be the head of our family?" to which Lillian replied, "Sometimes men don't listen to God very well and women have to lead."

Click! I stared at the phone I held in my hand and turned around towards the mirror to look at the expression on my face. I took a deep breath to calm myself.

Another disturbing connection I made was with another woman in Florida. We hit it off right away. I would never think that a relationship that far from California would work, but her photo and profile were very attractive. We exchanged many emails and she seemed eager enough, so we talked on the telephone a couple of times and things were going well. She only had one photo in her profile so I asked for additional photos and sent her some of mine. There was a pause in the action, then an email, apologizing.

"Dear Michael, Attached are the real photos of me. I posted a photo of my girlfriend because I did not want a photo of me on the Internet. Let me know, Abbie. "

I then wondered what else was untrue in her profile because she did not want it on the Internet. Had she posted her girlfriend's physical description, her girlfriend's ideas of a good time, her girlfriend's desires for a relationship? Maybe she posted her girlfriend's height and weight to make her a better catch. I looked over the photos attached as I thought. They showed a woman, alright, but not one I was ever going to be attracted to.

I wrote back. "*That is quite a shock, particularly after we talked about trust being the basis for relationships. Abbie, is your girlfriend available?*"

Okay, I didn't write that but I sure wanted to. I did ask her why she posted her girlfriend's photo and whether the girlfriend knew. It turned out that the girlfriend *did* know, and I ended up talking to her on the telephone that night. The two of them reasoned that it was the safe thing to do. Ugh!

New relationships are so fragile because we want to trust and want to believe in the basic goodness of humankind, but the disappointments just make us more cynical than we were when we started out.

I got smarter very fast after that. It turns out many people don't give real information online. One was a professional dominatrix who was looking for new clients; another was on welfare in Nova Scotia; another weighed over 300 pounds. I started asking all kinds of probing questions after the initial chit-chat. One woman confessed she was obese and added, "Don't worry, though, I know how to dress," then asked me out to go dancing.

Chapter Nine

Dinah, don't blow your horn

Looking for Mister Good
Age: 41
Height: 5' 7"
Body Type: Average
Hair Color: Brown

Dinah121

I'm a well-educated and adjusted woman who has had her hard times and is over them, but has learned a lot along the way. I love to laugh.

Occupation: Licensed Clinical Social Worker

Matches My Love Settings	....	☆☆☆
Matches My Distance Settings	....	-
Did She Match Her Profile	....	☆☆☆
Did She Match Her Photos	....	☆
Did We Have Fun	....	☆☆
Impression of Her as a Person	....	☆☆☆☆☆

"She is very intelligent"

What attracted me: She was a smart professional and interested in exploring life.

I chatted with or telephoned 30 to 40 women on ChristianMingle.com, including Dinah, from Ohio. Dinah was a social worker specializing in counseling people with addictions as part of a state recovery and welfare program. Her one photo showed her in a coat in autumn looking rather professional and very smart. I liked her bio, which had some key words that caught my attention.

In our conversations she indicated she was applying to a university in the Bay Area for some post-graduate work, which was encouraging to me. If I were to tell anyone that you could not fall in love on the phone, I would be lying – you can, and we did – well, at least it was infatuation. We talked about everything -- she was smart and could relate too much of what I was saying and I felt I understood her, as well. The more we got into emails and conversation, the more we talked about life, the future, sex and something we called "surrender."

It is kind of weird discussing sex and otherwise "kinky" information with someone you have never actually met, but we were developing a relationship, so it seemed important. After many phone calls, we became more and more intimate, as one conversation led to another, so to speak.

At that time I did not know exactly what that word "surrender" meant to this woman and I don't think she did either -- exactly. Part of the Christian culture I knew was the notion of separation of offices for husband and wife – you know, "The man rules the home" and all that -- when his wife lets him, anyway. But what I was beginning to understand is that some women deeply want to surrender to a man, and that rabbit trail goes very deeply into some kinky things such as spanking, domestic discipline, strict obedience and sexual voluntary love slavery.

I must admit, was very interested at first (blush, sweat). I imagined all the benefits to this lifestyle; then, I also imagined how much work it would be to run two lives. Oh my God, I thought, I have trouble enough running my own. I thought that in the extreme case I would be telling another fully-grown and capable adult what to do with her life. Now, that might make sense in a very traditional relationship and it even seemed to make some sense to me in a Christian relationship. However, the grand benefit in the larger sense might be that I get anything I want in the bedroom or any other room whenever I want and however I want. Wahoo! My horns went up – testosterone alert! Yet there's the rub. Just how was that going to work in real life? I do not want a doormat, but a sex slave? Well, maybe. I thought about it long enough to realize that it just wouldn't work for me, but it sure was interesting to talk about.

Again, I reflected back to my days at the OC when those girls seemed to lead all the guys around. Is this just another way of doing the same thing, I thought? Have grown women invented new tricks for guys my age, or is this the opportunity of a lifetime? Or, better yet, do females never really change?

Before half the world goes ballistic and the other half begins to empathize, I need to note that at that time it confused me that a self-proclaimed independent woman would want to be told what to do and then somehow enjoy it -- then it hit me -- well, at least I had one idea that seemed to make sense.

Perhaps "surrender" meant that when a woman is told what to do, it is safer and somewhat erotic; safer in that the woman is doing what someone tells her instead of making it up herself. She thinks, "He is the boss, after all, and he is telling me this, so it must be all right." Then, she gets erotic because it might be a ruse to get into a marriage -- then the hammer comes down – ouch!

My personal exploration of the topic of "surrender" started at that time as well. I knew about bondage, spanking and similar things from the Internet. It was something I found erotic and sexy, but I also found it dark and difficult, so I began to ask Dinah some questions. "What does surrender mean?" "How does it apply to different situations?" "Why is it attractive to you?" "Why is it a turn-on?" "Why am I uncomfortable with it, do you think?" "How does it fit with the rest of life, sex and the pursuit of happiness?"

Dinah's answers were surprising. She wanted it; the more we talked, the more she wanted. Wow, that is a lot just for phone calls and email. Someone I never met, someone I had known for just a few weeks, at a distance, was telling me some of the deepest, darkest secrets about herself. I think that maybe I got more than my toes wet in this deal.

As it turned out, I had to travel to Chicago for business purposes about once a month during this time, so I arranged to meet Dinah there. We agreed she would stay overnight if we liked each other. We would have coffee at the terminal and make plans to see the Metropolitan Art Museum the next day.

It was February in Chicago, there was snow on the streets, and I was there to help close a deal for a big project. I came dressed for the deal in a new suit, a great overcoat and very nice shoes, plus a fresh haircut and all the moxie I had expressed online. I was confident. I could dress to impress everyone. I was feeling great. I was dressed to kill. I even had on a new $200 tie.

After the business meetings, which lasted about six hours with all the trimmings, including presentations, questions and answers and a catered lunch, we closed the deal privately with the CIO and his team over drinks.

I sat with my colleagues in the Park Club overlooking Lake Michigan, sipping a glass of water and making small talk while they drank and celebrated the Michaely – I was in another world, one greater than money or Michaely -- in anticipation… just four hours from seeing Dinah for the first time.

Can you imagine the anticipation? It was terrifying, erotic, exhilarating and ever-so-difficult to focus. Finally the clock hit 6 p.m. I made my way to the train station in a cab with a printed picture of Dinah, a testosterone alert, and my best hello line practiced, rehearsed and ready to make a grand impression. My cab was early and her train was late. I got the unexpected pleasure of pacing to keep warm and stay cool, and then there she was.

Well. I'd like to say fireworks went off and we took a carriage ride through the park, but that did not happen. There are strange elements about people that create chemistry. For instance, if a woman dresses in a certain way or has a certain persona about her, there is a turn-on; and conversely, if she does other, certain things, flags go up – this can only be experienced; we all know the mystery of pheromones, of personal chemistry, that "connection," that indefinable "it." As it happened, "it" was not there. Sadly, chemistry isn't about coherent thought.

The initial experience was a real letdown (immediately; it's that sinking feeling you get in your gut when you know it's too late to run), but I was logical and ignored that feeling in favor of learning more about her, and how it was that I could be infatuated with a women I had never met. I chose to approach this intellectually.

She came in from the farthest terminal, so I watched as she approached and moved closer to her as she towed her baggage. This gave me a lot of time to look and think before we actually came together. She immediately reached out to embrace me and held me very tightly for a moment or two. Dinah was 5' 9" with an average to slender build, so her head was pressed to my neck and chest. I moved my cheek against hers, slowly moving her face towards mine from where it was focusing on my shoulder and then brought her lips towards mine and we passionately kissed – call it an experiment, but a tactical one -- to see how things went. Wow. That was the hottest way I ever started a coffee date.

She was dressed in winter clothes with fake-fur things to keep warm – you know, mitts, a hat and scarf and boots with heels. I took her mittened hand and we took the cab to a local Starbucks I had espied en route to the train station. We sat and talked a bit, having a few laughs and confessing our mutual anticipation. The coffee house was roasting hot – no pun intended -- as many establishments are in Chicago in winter, so we both began to peel off layers of clothing and soon were both comfortably sitting in daytime clothes, so I finally got my first look at her – nice, I thought.

We talked a bit further and both seemed to have a good time. The coffee date seemed successful so I asked if she would be staying, and she smiled and kissed me on the cheek so we layered back up and made the brief but cold cab ride to the Palmer House Hilton, where I was staying.

The lobby of the Palmer sure beat the train station décor; exotic murals were painted on a huge vaulted ceiling and lots of well-dressed people were milling about here and there. As we walked to the door, the bellhop took her bag and we strolled into that grand lobby. I think it must have been impressive because we went from holding hands to her taking my arm and walking very close to me as if she were proud as a pup.

The elevator ride to the executive floor increased the anticipation as the closeness continued and the bellhop smiled at us as if he knew our secret.

The room was also grand, well-furnished and quiet. The bellman put the suitcase on the bed, took his tip from my waiting hand, and exited without comment. Dinah inspected the room, touching things as if she were in some paradise, and then proceeded to arrange her things. I came up behind her like we were old lovers and began to kiss her neck while wrapping my arms around her front. Men look for signs of encouragement, and she encouraged me by wiggling her bottom in that special way, so the embrace led to some more embracing, kissing and small talk about dinner. Still aroused, we went off to dinner in the hotel's version of a pub.

What I noticed most about her was her nose; it was one of those eastern E-u-r-o-p-e-a-n noses. After getting used to that and still being in a semi-erotic mind-set while trying to remember to care about her feelings, I put that out of my mind and we have a great talk over dinner and drinks. Well, I admit that I watched as she moved her head back and forth, and she noticed too and talked about her heritage. We both had a couple of ales with dinner and began to loosen up while we chatted and laughed. After dinner, we walked around the lobby and through the galleries and shops, looking at the windows. I bought a Pendleton scarf at her suggestion, and then we returned to the room.

We kissed as we entered the room and she pushed me off and said she wanted to change for bed. I found that idea arousing and smiled as she turned and crossed the room toward her suitcase. She took some things into the bathroom – one of those old funky baths from the 1900s with white-everything and steam heat. She left the door open, and I could see her in the dressing mirror from my vantage point.

As she undressed, I noticed that even her panties and bra were leopard skin, just like her scarf and hat – oh, did I mention leopard skin? I sat on the edge of the thick down pillow-top bed and watched her. Then she excused herself and closed the door, emerging after 15 minutes. I took that time to don my running pants I brought to sleep in and a nice tee, and then I slipped under the covers.

It was all quite entertaining, yet a bit odd-feeling – like a dream or watching a movie. We knew each other, but we didn't. I had never been in a hotel room with a woman I just met, never had a rendezvous, no seedy sidewalk pickups, nothing.

She emerged from the closed door wearing a pale cotton gown falling just above the knees, and a bra and panties that I could see through the thin cloth. I kissed her and held her for a moment and then made a quick stop to brush my teeth and prepare for the night. While I was in the bathroom, she turned on some music and turned off the lights. When I returned, she was in bed, sitting up. I was definitely aroused.

We lay there in the dark and held each other, talking about this and that and much more about "surrender." I could feel her squirm when she talked to me in whispered tones about doing anything I wanted. Then the strangest thing happened -- I had a flashback of living at home as a kid, when that neighbor girl used to come into my room and lie back on the bed. I could never figure out what she was doing as we sat there, but suddenly, now I got it; she was waiting for me to start something at her invitation -- and so was Dinah – she wanted me to start.

I began to touch her, and then really touch her. I worked my magic until she was ready to burst, then stopped – her squirming was intense as she moved against my side. Unfortunately, we had agreed to not have sex on the first date. Why, I don't remember, but I lived up to my part, somehow, some way, in a heroic effort. Yes, somehow the most erotic thing was a feeling of power that came from her willingness to do whatever I asked, because she was so turned on. I touched her everywhere and she responded.

The next day we woke early – perhaps around 6:30. We snuggled together and began to repeat the performance of the night before, but then nature called us both so we took turns in the bathroom. Then she asked if she could shower before breakfast. "Please do, and could you leave the door open so I can watch?" I kidded deviously. She showered with the door open at my request – things were getting better and better. This voyeuristic thing was very appealing.

After I watched her dress and got dressed myself, we took an early breakfast in one of the hotel restaurants then a strolled a bit around the shops and lobby, having a second cup of coffee at the hostess bar – all the while talking and nudging each other. The power of arousal is huge, I thought. Around 10, after exhausting all the hotel shops and galleries we checked out and stowed our bags with the bell captain. We began the walk through the slush to a museum a few blocks away. The day was sunny and cold and she pulled me away from the building just in time to see a huge mass of ice fall from a tall overhang.

Dinah taught me about winters in the Midwest – apparently when the sun is out the ice falls, and wherever there are not ice guards or awnings on a building you get killed – who knew? I grew up in the rain. I had never even seen an icicle on a building that close-up.

The museum really had a great group of exhibits. We saw most of the first floor and basement before running out of time and gas. My favorite was the arts and crafts furniture exhibit, which showed enduring design in wooden chairs from American artists. We held hands as we strolled, talking about the art. For about an hour we sat in the garden restaurant looking out the window across the courtyard at the outdoor pristine winter scene – not a footprint or a bird was about, just the white and the ice and the barren trees. White draped everything except the icicles, which shimmered in the 1 p.m. sun that had begun to fade. I was tired; with the erotic tension and the slow strolling, it seemed like nap time to me. As 2:00 approached we took a cab to the train station, where we made a passionate kiss take a little longer than normal as I reached under her coat. I then hopped the orange-line to Midway and flew home. We kept up our calls and emails and arranged for her to come out to see me on Valentine's Day for an extended visit.

Chapter Ten

Mingling with Christians

It seems appropriate to let you in on a bit of my history to help you understand where all this comes from. At 17, I moved from Oregon to San Diego. The sun was a charm I was drawn to like a moth to fire. Oregon is a wet place most of the time, so sun and beaches looked good to a young, ambitious boy. There I found life very different from my small-town youth -- I found faith.

Christianity is full of exciting, interesting people – and yes, lots of women, too. For the first time the rules had changed for me. It was 1976 and I was the ripe old age of 18. There was no Internet, and because I had postponed school for the time being, meeting women was much harder. There was, however, Ruby the Filipina girl at the dry cleaners where we worked, but aside from her I didn't know another woman.

A friend invited me to a lecture on evolution and special creationism, so I went and my church life began. I joined many groups and made friends quickly, including many single women. The rules of Christianity were very different from my former free-spirited life. "No sex before marriage" was the mantra. You couldn't even touch them – gasp! Most of the girls I met were interesting to hang around with, but most of the singles were what I would later coin "lifetime singles." I formed a garage band in my spare time, which attracted a couple of girls, both of whom I was interested in.

I realized something pretty interesting about myself around this time: the more time I spent alone with a woman, the less likely it would be that we would NOT have sex. As a Christian, I justified that various kinds of sex were okay because they were not the kinds of sex that was taboo, and then I decided all sex was wrong until marriage. Then it was okay as long as you were going to get married. Man, it was mind-bending to deal with the rules and guilt. I was going mad trying to figure out what the rules were and why they existed. Meanwhile, there was a lot of touching going on and not much sex.

I lived in humble means in a part of town that would scare most people, so when I met Sheila I was immediately taken by the fact that she was so different from me. She was neat, organized and big-busted. Okay the busted part was not part of the neatness part, but it was pretty neat. Anyway, Sheila and I became inseparable and the more time we spent alone the more rules we broke. We did everything except you know what and I was feeling guilty and just hated it. Why should I feel guilt for wanting to, and for having sex? The guilt got to be too much, so Sheila and I solved that and got married.

The honeymoon was in Catalina, which turned out to be a mistake because their idea of a hotel room is like a Motel 6 – not very comfortable or romantic. Sheila was a virgin because we did not do it before marriage, and it was scary for her because it hurt -- so that moment lost all notion of being romantic. We rode horses, rented a go-cart, ate food, and did the same for several days, then that was it, our honeymoon.

We took an apartment near the university she attended. I worked doing whatever I could and we experimented with life, playing house and sex. It was during this time when I began to experiment with many things that would later become "dark" to me. I supposed many people were experimenting as well, but who in the world do you talk to about it in the Church? I can imagine the conversation with our youth pastor. "Pastor Bing? Ah, could I talk to you about bondage?" "Pastor Miller? Have you and your wife ever experimented with anal sex?" I don't think so. However, I would later learn that many Christian couples practice kinky sex.

The thought of the scene in *Harold and Maude* popped into my head where the pastor/priest was lecturing teenage Harold about getting married to the very old Maude. What a funny situation to be in -- nowhere to run, nowhere to hide.

Shelia and I broke up and got back together many times, and all the makeup sex was better than anything we had when we were together, so I was beginning to wonder if we should just break up all the time.

Afterthoughts: *"I have always been curious about the oddities in life, even those grotesque ones like vampires, because in being curious I remain teachable. That is important to me."*

Chapter Eleven

Valentine's Day

Dinah and I kept up our nightly conversations on the phone and still planned for her to fly out for Valentine's Day. We were hot for each other and the subject of "surrender" was heating up our lives more and more. I bought her a round-trip ticket and sent her some cash for expenses. When she arrived at the airport we took up right where we left off, and those darn flags went off again the moment I saw her outfit.

One of our conversations was, "What shall I wear for you when we meet?" I love women in summer dresses, but it was cold, so that wasn't practical. She once again wore her fake-fur scarf and had some fur around the handle of her suitcase. Something about that struck me as odd.

That day we took an early spring walk around the lake, holding hands and talking. My apartment was near a nice lake, and that time of year everything was green except the trees. That night we dressed to the Nines and took the train to San Francisco and dined at Morton's. Dinah was an intelligent woman, so our conversations were interesting. We shared some sautéed wild mushrooms and greens and ordered two of Morton's best steaks while we held hands, drank wine and talked.

That night was "interesting" – that's all I can say because I still was not committed, so I was not willing to go for it. She was enjoying her part immensely and I was having fun experimenting with "surrender." I had her do a strip tease, shower while I watched, dance for me, bow, kneel and on and on – wow, this was fun. Here was a woman who not only would do whatever I asked in the bedroom, but she loved it! I touched her where one finds those kinds of things out. I bent her over the bed while she was standing and deposited my fingers in all the places fingers go, and she had the time of her life. Her back arched, legs went ridged and she began to move in that way only a woman in heaven can. That went on for a good hour with moans of pleasure and instructions to move this way and that until she and my arm were exhausted. I'll bet years of pent-up desire dissipated just then for her – she was pink all over, panting and exhausted. We both collapsed into my bed.

The next day was Valentine's. We took a drive out to Santa Cruz and had lunch a nice restaurant on the main drag. While we ate, Van Morrison was playing on the restaurant sound system. I looked across at her, and she looked back at me with those gauzy, dreamy-filled eyes. I knew what that meant – here she was, gaga for me, and I was less committed than ever with her. It is funny how those things go. Here I could get whatever I wanted (presumably), and I did not want it that much. My thoughts ran back to just how much work it would be to run my life and someone else's too. Just what did I want, then? Could I get it? Was Dinah the one to give it to me? Ah, those questions again.

After a beautiful drive up the coast, seeing the ocean at its best, azure green where the sun hit the water and the bloom of wild flowers that grace the hills that time of year, we ended back at my place. I turned on some Van Morrison and ran a hot bath with body oil and salts mixed in, threw in some rose petals from the flowers I greeted her with, lit a few candles and asked her to do a sexy strip tease and then get into the bath. She was more than willing and gave a stellar performance, touching herself here and there as she shed her clothes. She soaked for about 45 minutes while I came in and out. I spent plenty of time washing her slowly; she was ready to burst again.

While she soaked, I had made some fresh fare: cold meats and bit-sized sweets on a plate. She emerged from the bath in just a white towel. We sat close and sampled the food. I poured some plum wine – very sweet; then our conversation returned to surrender and sex again, at her direction. Dinah was squirming in the chair as she talked and asked me to command her to do things. While I enjoyed her company, I was not interested in extending our relationship. I realized that her asking to be commanded reminded me of a similar kind of passive-aggressive behavior I had lived with before. So, because I did not want to hurt her feelings on this special day, I took her by the towel forcefully to the beat of Van singing, ripped off the towel, turned her around facing away from me, bent both of her arms behind her back and bent her over the bed with force and did a repeat performance. She was in ecstasy, making all her love sounds. I was not.

I turned the heat up in the apartment so she could remain naked as I had her pose for me (I got a kick out of that as it was very artistic) – that part of the proposition I enjoyed because it was like playing charades – making art or being someone else for a moment. We watched a movie in between poses and then fell asleep. The next day I put her on the plane and never saw her again.

Notes to self: There is some merit and even bravery to "surrender," but chemistry is more important, and Dinah was exactly the kind of woman I had been attracting since the beginning. I found the topic of surrender interesting, erotic and new and wanted to know more about it. Just how many women like that sort of thing anyway? I was confused by the surrender and asking paradox -- who was exactly in charge when she was getting what she wanted? Well, I did get to experiment. Even so, I was looking for more of a real connection because falling in love is such fun -- everyone should do that regularly.

I pulled my ad on ChristianMingle.com, vowed never to use a Christian dating site again, reformulated my ad and signed up at Yahoo! personals. Wow, that was strange and fun. I was still a Christian but wasn't interested in looking for Christian women in particular; I just did not want to attract that kind of woman -- it felt a little like bait and switch. You know when the ad gets you into the store and then you get switched to the more expensive item, or worse, they lie and say they didn't have the one you wanted in stock? I decided that all that talk about surrender would have evaporated in a kind of passive-aggressive behavior later when she was not getting what she wanted, and it would take a lot of effort to live with it.

Afterthoughts: *"For Valentine's Day and all days when romance is on my mind I just focus my affection on my partner, and romance finds its way into your day."*

"It is not my goal to sleep with every woman I date. Like many women, I get an emotional attachment from sex so I reserve it for women I care for deeply."

Chapter Twelve

What women want
(Christian women, that is)

After the experience with Dinah, I sat at my desk and ate tablespoons of peanut butter, savoring them in mouth to make myself feel better. I'd make faces of satisfaction while I wondered how Dinah felt at that moment. Peanut butter is my comfort food of choice, so Skippy extra-creamy made my day as I thought about things.

I thought about the fact that I had dated or married several Christian women by this time in my life and had many friends who were Christians. I had this mental image of Christian behavior -- wives submitting to their husbands as they would to Christ – that was not my experience. In addition, this surrender thing looked like my mental image of a traditional relationship: you know, a woman in a dress greeting her husband with a hot meal and a kiss each night.

I thought about it, then that argument that haunted me crossed my mind again: What if they are not submitting to Christ? Christian women want what many women want -- they want love and security, a good life and a nice sex life, but they seem in large number to want to resist any kind of leadership because they actually want to be an equal partner, not a submissive or whatever you call it. You know, I am the leader as long as she lets me – there's the rub. Christianity was just not working for me here. I asked questions about this to those I could question but got blank stares back.

I was left with a great deal of confusion. Was there a woman who was Christian who was not like that? How do I figure that out? Was I not enough of a leader to warrant a long-term relationship where it worked? I could see the game, just like at OC where the women were actually in control and knew how to lead men into God knows what, but my experience told me that was not real, it would not last, it was just the bait, then you get the switch after you are married.

I did not want to spend the rest of my life attending marriage encounters learning to live in perfect harmony with my wife, who was supposed to be the woman I wanted to start with. I can't imagine what possessed me to even consider being in a relationship that took that much work.

Then a larger question arose: If that was the bait, why couldn't I fish without being caught myself? That bait was nice, I would like that, but I would miss what I thought I wanted in a soul mate. Could I get women to show that bait all the time? It seemed the better way to me but I reminded myself that I was looking for a soul mate and in general, women wanted to have a relationship.

Christian women worked hard at the attracting part but not very hard at the keeping end of the deal. I realized it was time to start thinking about this differently. I knew there must be a compromise here, but not with myself, rather with the idea I was going to do all the work -- you know, the chase. I liked it better when both of us were chasing.

The engineer in me could not quite come up with a formula to make this work, so I reasoned it must be a matter of the heart. "Abandon all hope all ye who enter here," I thought, remembering Dante and his inferno. I needed a drink, a bigger pool of friends, and some advice from someone who had actually had sex once in their life other than the traditional missionary position.

POPULAR MEETING PLACE

Chapter Thirteen

My best thinking on MLRs and FLRs

After meeting Dinah, who arguably should have been a dream come true for some guy, I began to think a great deal about the nature of relationships. It seemed to me that programming had a lot to do with relationships. You know, the programming we get growing up and observing.

Here I had assumed that traditional relationships worked in a specific way, and I was not sure where exactly I learned that. Males, I assumed, led relationships in a traditional setting. I assumed that females wanted it that way. So how were my ideas of traditional relationships any different from reality, especially after what I experienced with Christian dating?

Then, being the good student of philosophy that I am, I reversed it, now asking the question, What about Female-Led Relationships? Were FLRs the opposite of Male-Led Relationships only by virtue of gender? The espoused ideal of equals in a relationship, I reasoned, is a tough way of doing things because of the troubles inherent in equality. And if so many women want the traditional relationship of the strong male leader, then why do relationships fail so often when there *is* a strong male leader?

I thought back to all my relationships, looked at my friends, and I had serious doubts if there was such a thing as an equal relationship. I seemed that most relationships that *looked* equal seemed more like roommate situations than marriages. My own experience looked like the brow-beaten male led by his dominant wife or the overbearing male leader, the traditional Christian man who "ruled" his home, but that was about it.

When I was young I never gave any thought to these kinds of things. Relationships were all about attraction and availability and things just seemed to work out – for a while, at least – but fast-forward to now, and I thought about them a lot. Why the hell don't they have relationship courses in school? Who wrote the book of love? Who made the rule that men were leaders? Was this nature or nurture? Well, enough ranting... I was thinking hard on the subject and coming to some startling conclusions.

The first thing that became clear to me was that couples do not seem to talk about or define how their relationships will go for them. When I discussed it with them they joked about it, made some male or female-bashing comments or just looked at me with a blank stare. They talked around the subject but not *about* it. So if people don't really get into a discussion about what they expect from their mate beforehand – and Lord knows I never did -- was this the reason relationships failed? The guy just assumes he will rule? The woman assumes she will be "taken care of?" What is equal anyway? Why would a guy *want* to be equal to a woman, for that matter? Aren't we supposed to be different?

The second thing that struck me was that people don't spell out their expectations exactly to their mates until much later in a relationship, and then only because of the disappointment of not getting something they wanted. At that point it seems more like nagging than discussing differences. Perhaps people are just not that

good about communication and by the time they get
around to it, it takes a lot of work.

One of my good friends appeared to have a happy
marriage, so I asked him and his wife separately about it.
They said they had made a deal that he would lead and
she would follow. I asked her how she felt about that,
and she was good with it. So smart people *did* talk about
it – sometimes. I knew I needed to build that into my plan
if I was going to build a lasting relationship, but my
questions were just creating more questions in my mind.

My boss is a friend of mine and also a woman. One day
we had a conversation over drinks in which she intimated
that it was not about equality, it was about roles. "Must
be too much whisky," I thought to myself. "There's no
difference."

In her version of an ideal relationship, people operated
within their strengths. For example, if she was better at
dealing with money, she handled the finances, and if he
was, he did. I asked her how that worked for her and
she said, "Not very well – but it *should* work like that." I
chuckled a little as to not offend her. I never heard her
say anything positive about the subject.

So the prevailing wisdom is that people share roles? Max
was a professional money manager, but his wife did the
family finances; Alexis was a human resources executive
who was getting a divorce because her husband cheated
on her. Well, that burned that theory. It seemed more like
the person doing the job was available, interested, so
they did it, and I doubt either of them discussed it.

I thought it had to be better to get the ideal design for
relationships out there somewhere near the beginning so

it can be discussed right away, at the onset. A designed relationship made sense to this project manager.

Afterthoughts: *"I met a couple who shared the secret of their successful relationship with me. They said, "Both partners need to be forgiving. Both partners need to be genuinely nice people and both partners need to have a very short memory of pain and a long memory of pleasure."*

Chapter Fourteen

Yahoo!

Compared to Yahoo, ChristianMingle is extremely small. Yahoo had thousands of women in my locale, and many of them were attractive and interesting. I created my ad after carefully rewording it to reflect what I learned on ChristianMingle, loaded my photos and paid the bill – net charges $129 for a premium account for three months. By that time I'd used my digital camera many times and had a variety of photos I felt represented me well. I am a tall, attractive guy, and women seem to find me attractive, especially my eyes, so I cropped a photo to accentuate my eyes.

Yahoo has an announcement service, and man, does it work. I got hundreds of responses from all over the Bay Area and beyond: professional woman, public servants, school teachers, health care professionals, and so on, by the score. The first woman I connected solidly with was Tammy:

Life is too short
Age: 46
Height: 5' 11"
Body Type: Average
Hair Color: Blond (Oh really)

HorseLady77

As a hard-working woman, I also take time to play. I would love to share some special time with someone who enjoys what I do.

Occupation: Technical Project Manager

Matches My Love Settings	....	☆☆☆☆☆
Matches My Distance Settings	....	☆☆☆☆☆☆
Did She Match Her Profile	....	☆☆☆☆☆☆
Did She Match Her Photos	....	☆☆☆☆☆☆
Did We Have Fun	....	☆☆
Impression of Her as a Person	....	☆☆☆☆☆

"Horse people – go figure"

What attracted me: She was good-looking and in the same field I am in.

Tammy lived in Pleasanton – a nearby city. She was the first woman I'd met online who was not from the Christian community. She was in tech, so we had things in common right off, and she also shared her love of horsemanship. She was a definite horse person.

We met in Pleasanton for the first time after several days of email exchanges. Tully's is a local landmark. A coffee shop frequented by people who ride Harleys – you know, motorcycles. Nowadays, lots of average citizens and rich men ride them instead of the bikers of the '60s and '70s. The dot.com success crowd and professionals have taken over and are now riding them. So, Tully's was full of would-be bikers.

Tammy was easy to spot and I found her with ease. We smiled at each other and ordered some coffee then sat outside, which, at Tully's, is an experience in itself given all the motorcycles. We hit it off in our conversations about travel and the outdoors, then decided to walk around and ended up at a local bar in a restaurant and had drinks. As we talked in the dimly lit room, I reached across and touched her hands. They were calloused because she was a horse person and it naturally took a toll on her skin. Normally I'd take her pulling back as a warning flag, but because her hands were calloused I thought she may have been self-conscious about them, so I ignored the flag. But I took note of it.

We emailed and called each other several times and she offered to take me on a trip to Carmel, which is about an hour and thirty minutes south by car. Carmel is a fantastic city and I had never been, so I was looking forward to seeing this great city full of art and restaurants.

We met at Starbucks early on a Saturday morning on a cool but very sunny day. Carmel is a city of art, shops, the beach and nice restaurants, and Tammy knew it well, so she gave me the dime tour. The drive from took us through the country and some interesting artichoke-growing regions until you get to the coast at seaside, so we chatted and listened to music – all in all a comfortable ride. Parking in Carmel on Saturday can be an adventure, but we found a spot just six blocks off the main street, where we went for breakfast at a local eatery, the Benedict Café.

The restaurant was one of those famous family owned joints, and they had 20 to 30 kinds of Benedicts. Tea drinkers are a special breed of women, so when she ordered herbal tea with her Lobster Benedict, I registered another red flag. She also seemed a bit awkward; I got the sense that she needed some space between herself and the rest of the world.

We walked the shops and galleries after eating. Carmel is wonderful like that, with lots of windows and open doors. Tammy carried this enormous bag, like the kind mothers carry, with her. The shops are sometimes small, and one of them specialized in expensive glass art. We went in, with her enormous bag -- every time she turned I cringed because the bag grazed a glass bowl, sculpture or piece of art. The price of one bowl the purse disturbed was $12,000 – I thought to myself, I'll bet the contents of that bag and the bag are less than $500. I decided to seek our entertainment elsewhere before it cost me my kid's education fund.

All day as we walked in the romance of Carmel, I attempted to make contact in friendly man-woman ways -- you know, bumping softly as we joked, a light touch, holding hands. No matter what I did, or how innocent it was, she would have none of it. I was discouraged, but we were in Carmel, and at least I began a romance with that place – even if it was going to have to be by myself.

As the day began to end, we ate dinner at Little Napoli, a nice Italian restaurant, and made the long drive home. The drive was nice; we talked about many things. After we arrived back, I attempted a kiss, but she was not interested.

Oddly, she asked for another date as I walked her to her car. "When do you want to get together again?" she said, easing into her car seat. I replied, "Let's chat about it." I went home and amended my ad the moment I booted up my computer: "I am an affectionate man. I love to hold hands, rub your shoulders and look into your eyes." Next...

Then there were a series of misadventures and hopeful moments.

Breaker Breaker
Age: 44
Height: 5' 9"
Body Type: Slender
Hair Color: Brown

SurferGirlsLove
Hi guys. I'm in love with anything to do on or in the water. I'm tall and slender and still surf when I get a chance. Let's go for it.

Occupation: Surf Shop Owner

Matches My Love Settings	....	☆☆☆☆☆
Matches My Distance Settings	....	☆☆☆☆☆
Did She Match Her Profile	....	☆☆☆☆☆☆
Did She Match Her Photos	....	☆☆☆☆☆☆
Did We Have Fun	....	☆☆
Impression of Her as a Person	....	☆

"Board – no pun intended"

What attracted me: Her photos

Meet Sally, the surf shop owner. She and I had the outdoors in common, and because she was a surfer chick, I figured I'd really enjoy meeting her. We met on her commute home from work to her home, which I was surprised to find was such a long distance. She was very relaxed and slouched back in the chair as we drank coffee and talked.

The conversation went to her past relationship, which was fair game because of our interest in a relationship. It turned out her ex-husband had been in the carpet business, and so had I. She stood up and said she was not interested in learning that information. Perhaps it solidified something she was already feeling – strikeout.

I sent some flowers to her business the next day and a card, which read, "I smile when I remember our meeting." To this day, I am still not sure what that meant.

Linda worked for a utility email company. We decided to meet at a local Starbucks because she lived nearby. She arrived earlier than I did and came to the coffee shop with a book. I arrived and looked around the room I was very familiar with, but saw no one looked who resembled the photos I saw on the web. However, I noticed one woman reading and just assumed it was her. That must have been a really good book because she never looked up to see if I was there, so I just sipped my coffee and watched her, then left.

She wrote again later, wondering why I did not show up. I asked what book she was reading. She asked for another chance. I wrote, "Pass." I could imagine a date in which she read the entire time, through dinner, then through the theater, then through the first kiss.

Lets celebrate life together
Age: 47
Height: 5' 10"
Body Type: Slender
Hair Color: Blond (maybe?)

LegallyBlond108

I love rollerblading around the lake and getting outdoors. I have a couple of kids at home still. I am very outgoing and I love to be around other active people.

Occupation: Legal Secretary

Matches My Love Settings	....	☆☆☆☆
Matches My Distance Settings	....	☆☆☆☆☆☆
Did She Match Her Profile	....	☆☆☆
Did She Match Her Photos	....	☆☆☆☆☆
Did We Have Fun	....	☆☆☆☆☆
Impression of Her as a Person	....	☆☆☆☆☆

"A kiss gone bad"

What attracted me: Her photos, her positive attitude, and great phone calls.

Brenda was a looker -- tall and lean with a beautiful face and figure, full of life. She was the daughter of Mormon parents and lived with her kids in the next town over. In one of our many email exchanges, she shared that she was a legal secretary -- wow, and smart as a whip, too. We met up at the nearest Starbucks, and she came to coffee fully equipped in a mini skirt and tight shirt. Swing!

She lit up the room, and we talked for some time until our coffee was almost gone. I never knew if she planned it but her skirt was so short I could see her panties, which flashed their special message several times at me.

"Sexy" surrounded by a heart was printed on them. I always wondered if that was a test to see if I would look. If I looked, would she think I was interested, or was she testing me to see if I was just in it for sex? Was I a good candidate because of my chaste behavior? As the date ended, I walked her to her car and said, "There is something I'd like to try," as I stood within a foot of her, face-to-face. The slope of the road was perfect, as we were almost lip-to-lip in height. "May I kiss you?" I asked. She nodded elegantly and closed her eyes as I got closer. I kissed her with a little passion but mostly in a friendly way, and she responded. After getting home, she sent me an email and said she had decided to give up dating for a while because she was not ready emotionally. Strike three. You are out!

Chapter Fifteen

Scanning Ads

For better or worse, online ads are the way many of today's singles meet, and despite my "bad luck" thus far, I have to admit, I was getting very good at scanning them.

I knew that men don't get anywhere near the attention women get, so I tended to cruise ads and send emails to the ones who seemed attractive and interesting. One woman said she got hundreds of inquiries and almost never answered them unless she was attracted to the photos. Competition, I thought. Hundreds of eligible men all looking at the same woman, and then there was me.

I decided photos were not enough to beat the competition because women are attracted to a variety of men, and even some men I find unattractive. I realized I needed the right words. Women like words. I needed to be able to scan an ad, think of the right thing to say, and communicate it on a genuine level.

I began to categorize the kind of ads I saw by the leading paragraph and moniker, or "handle," as they call it, if there was one. I avoided any ad where the woman started out by talking about her body. Phrases like, "I am petite but curvy," "My best feature is my smile," and "My best feature is my youthful appearance" seemed like dead giveaways for insecurities or pure vanity. Lots of people dislike their bodies – maybe most of us, I reasoned, but why talk about it first? I thought leading in with insecurities was a mistake.

Statements like "I don't want to rush in," "Let's take our time," and "I like a slow hand" seemed like hints about women getting over pain or not looking for a long-term relationship. "I am looking for friends" seems to mean she was not looking for a relationship, but just to date. The killers of all correspondence were ads that had phrases like "This seems weird to me," "I am new to online dating," "A friend of mind suggested I try this," or "I don't really know what to say here."

Women who led with their ethnicity gave me red flags too, because I could not understand why they did this unless they were looking for the same ethnicity in a man. "I am a Filipina-American," "I was born in Brazil," "I am German by birth." "My ancestry is Russian/Austrian."

Also, the old "SWF" still showed up way too often. Of course I'll realize at least that you're white and female; come on, throw me a bone! Then there was "I was born here and lived here all my life." That did not sound like she had a very *interesting* life.

There are many women who led with, "Single mom," "I love Family," "Mom of three kids," "I have a great family," "My kids are my life," or "Soccer mom." It seemed to me that these women felt a guy must want kids to want them or perhaps they were looking for the next hubby after the last hubby. Either way it did not make sense because the relationship must first exist between the man and woman, then the kids – right? If it was about the kids, then why not have the kids troll for a dad?

I could always tell what a woman lacked in her past relationship when she put it right out there saying, "I'd like a guy who can be real and genuine," "Someone who shares my values," "Nice guy with no vices," "Being true to myself." This looked a good approach in getting what she wanted, but why place it up there so high in the ad? I believe in telling people what you are looking for and that you have been hurt, but I noticed many ads started with descriptions of romance that seemed a bit off. "I am a hopeless romantic." And "Looking for that special someone" seemed a bit impersonal; did she look to everyone for romance?

I would never answer an ad that said "I want a man to complement my life" or "I am looking for a man who knows how to be a man." What in the world does that mean? Complement, as in "Your life is so nice today, darling, now that I'm with you," or "I just love the way your life looks in this light. It matches mine!"

Okay, that was sarcastic and a bit raunchy, I admit it and apologize for it, but it does make a good point. By the way, if you are going to be the judge of what makes a man a man, then you'd better be ready for a surprise: men come in all types, shapes and sizes, and that statement will scare away most men because "What makes a man a man after all?" It's another one of those indefinable "it's!"

The best ads gave me something to ask about, something to connect with, like: "I love flowers," not just "I love life." "I read poetry" not just, "I love to read a good book." Vague ads like "I love to laugh" gave no entry to a conversation; is there anyone who does not think they love to laugh? The old, "I love to have fun and am looking for a man to enjoy life with" did not really say anything interesting, either. It just didn't give me anything to respond to.

All right, here is a good shot at an ad that attracted me. "I am a dichotomy: independent but enjoy intimate company, a free thinker but a good listener, love nature and opera." She went on to say, "There must be a man like me, who loves both traveling and staying at home, romance and rabid sex." Now, that gave me some things to talk about. I could talk about my last kayaking trip to the Trinities or the last opera I saw. I could lead by asking questions about what she liked in nature, or if she like gardens. These thoughtful ads made it easier for me, and I appreciated it.

Chapter Sixteen

The School Teachers

I was on Match.com and Yahoo by then and trying out some new ad words when I met several school teachers – fourth, fifth, and sixth grade, respectively.

Looking for someone to smile with
Age: 47
Height: 5' 5"
Body Type: Average
Hair Color: Black

lovelylady99

I am a little shy but still adventurous. I like trying new things and travel. I am hoping to meet a nice man to share time and travel with.

Occupation: School Teacher

Matches My Love Settings	....	☆☆☆
Matches My Distance Settings	....	☆☆☆☆☆
Did She Match Her Profile	....	☆
Did She Match Her Photos	....	☆
Did We Have Fun	....	☆
Impression of Her as a Person	....	☆

"My grandma's apprentice"

What attracted me: She lived nearby

At first I was interested until I discovered her fetish was to go on cruises. Oh well, I got a cup of coffee, right? I always associated cruises with my grandma, so I moved on after the coffee was gone.

launalane

Hummmmmmmmmmmmmm!
Age: 50
Height: 5' 5"
Body Type: Few extra pounds
Hair Color: Light Brown

I am new at this; my friends said it was fun. So please be gentle. I think what I want is to find a best friends to do things with.

Occupation: School Teacher

Matches My Love Settings	....	☆☆☆
Matches My Distance Settings	....	☆☆☆☆☆
Did She Match Her Profile	....	☆
Did She Match Her Photos	....	☆
Did We Have Fun	....	☆
Impression of Her as a Person	....	☆

"Shhhhh! I am shy"

What attracted me: She contacted me.

She was quiet, shy, and hardly said a word. I think some women are just shell-shocked by personal contact, but when alone with a computer they are pure animals at sending email – uninhibited by the gaze of another. Human contact seems much more complex than emailing.

Let's go hiking!
Age: 44
Height: 5' 4"
Body Type: Slender
Hair Color: Blond (I don't think so!)

kthrou50

I am a straightforward woman. I like real people. I am goal-oriented and like to make things happen.

Occupation: School Teacher

Matches My Love Settings	....	☆☆☆☆
Matches My Distance Settings	....	☆☆☆☆
Did She Match Her Profile	....	☆☆☆☆☆
Did She Match Her Photos	....	☆☆☆☆☆
Did We Have Fun	....	☆☆☆☆☆
Impression of Her as a Person	....	☆☆☆☆

"Wow – energetic and sexy"

What attracted me: Her photos, her positive attitude, and our phone calls were great.

Emmy and I met for coffee and took a walk around the lake. She was 5' 4" and very attractive. I, on the other hand am 6' 4", so that was a bit awkward – but most of my female relationships have been with women from 5" 4" to 5' 7", so I thought nothing if it. Plus, I could pick her up, which would be nice at certain erotic moments.

Emmy was a beautiful, healthy woman with a passion for life. Her eyes sparkled when she talked, and she kept herself in shape. She spent some effort on surgical tweaks to her figure, which definitely spoke for itself, and aside from the physical attraction she was bright and personable – interesting to talk to.

We dated several times. On our first date she pressed in for the kill. She was very sexual and I was not ready. Don't laugh; I may be the only guy on earth who does not want to sleep with every girl he meets. I want to know them first because of those little fears of getting a gift that keeps on giving – there are too many men with lasting reminders of one-night-stands, and I don't want to be one of them.

I am a clever boy, so I took control and she loved it. She came over and sat on my lap and began passionately kissing me. Her size being what it was, I stood up with her wrapped around me and said "We are going to play a game. The rules are, you are going to do anything I want." I knew this tactic would not work with just anyone, and very likely it would have scared more timid women, but Emmy was hot for it and I could tell she enjoyed games. It is an erotic game and fun to play "control." I told her my plan: "I am going to shower you, give you a luscious, full-body massage and then what ever comes up – well, we'll see."
With her still clinging to me, I walked to the bedroom as we kissed passionately. I stood her in front of me and set her down without missing a kiss. I took her arms and held them behind her back as she struggled against me, then walked around her and pressed her arms between me and her so she got the point that they were to stay there. Slowly I unbuttoned her blouse and ran my hands across her skin, kissing her neck and pressing her close. Eventually we ended up against the wall, where she was pressed between me and it. She was lost in that moment of passion and began to melt to anything I was doing. I took off her clothes slowly and touched her in all the right ways, then washed her from the neck down in the shower, taking my time teasing her.

After the shower I dried her and carried her to the bed where I warmed some lotion between my hands and massaged her while tantalizing and kissing her body. She was in the zone. I let my fingers do the talking -- three times she exploded and exclaimed that was the first she ever had three. She offered reciprocation, but I said this time was it was just for her.

We dated again – this time for a hike and a drive down the coast, ending at a fish house before returning to her condo. San Francisco is a gorgeous place for hiking, and I chose Muir Woods, which is challenging to hike and filled with the beauty of ancient trees, wild iris and awesome views of the ocean. The drive down the coast was very nice, the flowers were in bloom and the sun shined on the water, making it azure and gray. A storm had passed through days earlier, and the water was churning and wonderfully foamy. We stopped here and there and enjoyed the very scenic day holding hands and embracing, bumping shoulders and stealing an occasional kiss.

Finally, after two-thirds of the day had passed, we made our way back to her condo where I had picked her up early that morning. Inside I saw for the first time her décor. Everything was very neat, and she had some very charming art displayed in several places. I sat on the couch with the water she had served me while she discreetly slipped into the next room and came back wearing less than she had on when she had left. Then she sat directly in my lap in that state of undress – I must be crazy, but I passionately kissed her, stood up without her ever detaching her from me, walked coupled as we were to her bedroom, deposited her on her bed, did a repeat performance and left without committing myself

My First 32 Coffee Dates

further. Next! Emmy needed a 19-year-old guy who just wanted to do it! A guy my age would be hard-pressed to be her companion. Her drive was such that I would not be able to trust that she would be able to maintain an exclusive relationship.

I broadened my search by using more websites with different ads to see which was most effective. One ad was designed to find very independent women; one to find more interested in surrender; and still another was for someone like me, but female. I tried match.com; perfectmatch.com; eharmony.com; cupid.com; and alt.com for starters. Match and Yahoo offered the biggest pool, and I was slow to get going with eHarmony.com, which was supposed to provide better fits for my personality.

Afterthoughts: *"I learned not to stereotype women by meeting so many; they are all different and interesting and I learned so much from them – I am grateful."*

83

Chapter Seventeen

Words and activities, anyone?

I am an active guy, and doing things makes we feel good about life. They don't have to be exotic or far away, and they don't have to be expensive or elaborate, but those things are good too.

When I look at a woman's personal ad (aside from the pictures), the only thing I have to judge her by is her words, so if there are too few, I'd be reluctant to contact her. On the other hand, if there are too many I'd be afraid of her being a control freak, so where to draw the line? And what's in a word anyway?

I noticed that women tended to exaggerate about their activities. If I asked about camping because I saw it in her ad, she'd say she loves to camp, then I would ask when was the last time she camped and, she'd respond, "A couple of years ago." Then, if I asked for more details, it would turn out to be *many, many* years since she camped, or she only went a couple of times and it was always with a camper van. It seems the devil is in the details. Words just don't mean what I might think they should.

For example, there was another ad from a woman who "loved the arts" but could not tell me one event she'd been to. And there was the woman who said she loved water sports but had only been one time -- when she was a girl. The woman who loved dining out never mentioned a nice restaurant, and all those women who love sunsets and walks on the beach almost never go. Now, I love flowers and birds, and I observe flowers and birds as often as I can – probably hundreds of times each year -- so I figured my definition of love just must not be the same as others'.

In kindness to the truth, not all ads are like that, and asking questions is certainly fair game. The women I have discussed this with get hundreds of hits from men and often are fishing for someone who is not a couch potato, so they try to find the things they did not have in their past relationships. Kind of like the way Debbie was fishing.

Debbie was a smart woman I never met face-to-face, but we spent lots of time exchanging emails. Marketing people usually know a lot about words, and she did. She was on Yahoo and Match.com and got hundreds of hits -- most of which did not pan out. She was a marketing executive with an Internet company and traveled a great deal, so any relationship she had would have to be in her downtime. Debbie had also just come out of an unhappy, seemingly endless 15-year marriage.

Debbie's ad was interesting and her photos were of her in various settings of happy scenes. One photo was her with a girlfriend at what looked like a beach setting, and the caption said "Aloha," so I could have assumed it to be in Hawaii, but it was not. Another was of her and two other good-looking friends in what looked like a courtyard in a foreign city with the caption "Bonaventure," which might have meant she was traveling in a foreign country, but it didn't. She was pictured skiing, biking, dining and dressed for a formal event.

What I later understood was that all these images were from her life as a married woman within the last five years -- events she attended without hubby number two.

She was serious about projecting an image she thought an active-minded man would want.

Her skiing picture was not her; her aloha friends were at a business retreat in Santa Cruz; and the foreign country was in the courtyard of a museum with her marketing team during a convention in San Diego.

In some ways, I had to hand it to her -- Debbie was an expert at image-making; she did it for a living, after all. She also presented it to the men who looked at her ad, including me. I wondered if she ever found a way to explain the deception to a man as they were falling in love. If not, she would have most certainly carried an untruth into a new relationship. By the way, her handle was, "Are you my wild one?"

PEOPLE OF DIFFERING REALITIES

Chapter Eighteen

Ladies from Marin County

Marin is the county and planet just north of San Francisco City over the Golden Gate Bridge. The place is famous for liberal politics, rich people and a natural lifestyle. The demographics of those who live in Marin County is often on the rather "well-to-do" side because housing prices are so high. The women there have a reputation for being interestingly different.

Marin is famous for being home to George Lucas of *Star Wars* fame, Birkenstocks™, and Autodesk, the makers of Autocad®. The place is beautiful, green, temperate and also a place where higher rates of depression and cancer occur than in any other part of the Bay area – like I said, this place is like "another planet."

Tall drink of water!
Age: 51
Height: 5' 10"
Body Type: Slender
Hair Color: Blond (no way!)

toocoolforwords

Be real, I am hit on a lot, so if you contact me
be someone real with something real to say.
I am a model who loves sensual massage
and fireside glasses of wine.

Occupation: Model

Matches My Love Settings	....	☆☆☆
Matches My Distance Settings	....	☆☆
Did She Match Her Profile	....	☆☆
Did She Match Her Photos	....	☆☆☆☆☆
Did We Have Fun	....	☆☆
Impression of Her as a Person	....	☆☆

"Looks great hanging on your arm"

What attracted me: Her photos.

One of the most interesting women I met would curl your
hair. She had a great photo display along with her profile.
She was a fashion model who, though not yet 50, was
doing older women's ads and some glamour work, which
she included in her profile. She was on Yahoo and lived
in Marin County, which, as I alluded to slightly before,
has a reputation for attracting some of the oddest-
behaving people, and some of the nicest, as well, so it
seemed like a crap shoot to me. How could I go wrong?
It might be an adventure.

I emailed her and gave her my best shot with some kind words and included something about myself and what I liked about her ad. She was slow in responding at first, but not because she was shy. She was popular and getting hit on by many other guys. I honestly did not think I had a chance, so when she responded I took note and my self-confidence crept up a notch.

She agreed to meet me for coffee after several email exchanges. Marin is quite a drive for me so I made it part of my work day, which already had me in San Francisco. At 5 p.m. we met in Mill Valley. "Wow" cannot describe her. She was tall and lean and had a face to write home about. Mill Valley is a four-corner town, and each one of the corners has a coffee shop. We drank coffee and laughed; she was very affectionate and got closer as we talked. Out of the blue she suggested we have dinner, which we did at an Italian restaurant on corner two. She was open and affectionate and walked across the street on my arm; she made me feel like she was proud for me to be there – and I felt special that I had her attention. She had a certain sashay in her step which kept us in physical contact.

From that time on, we had good physical chemistry, and it felt nice, warm and friendly, so after a nice meal, we went for drinks and dessert at a combo restaurant and bar next to the coffee shop just across the street.

The waitress in the bar was young and fair. I ordered a coffee and a pastry. The model just ordered a malt whisky. The waitress served my tart and coffee quickly, but she took a long time serving the whisky so we made small talk and picked at the tart while we waited.

Finally we flagged her down and asked about the drink. Then the waitress talked with me for a minute about something. The model spoke very loudly to the waitress in no uncertain terms to "Stop flirting with my date, and get me the damn drink I ordered." Then she turned to me and smiled and resumed our conversation as if nothing had happened. I asked her why she was cross with the waitress and she explained that it was clear the waitress was flirting and showing cleavage, and that was not her job. I hadn't noticed the flirting or cleavage earlier, but then I started looking!

Afterwards, as we walked together to my car, she was on my arm and very close. As we got to my car she pushed me onto the hood affectionately and firmly planted herself atop me and passionately kissed me as if she were staking claim and were about to have sex right there – that was wild, and most arousing, I have to admit. But I drove away saying in my head as I passed over the Golden Gate Bridge, "That woman is trouble I don't need." We never connected again. In hindsight, I think she was trying to show me what I was going to be missing.

When the Roses Bloom We Are There!!
Age: 44
Height: 5' 5"
Body Type: Average
Hair Color: Brown

greenthumb007
I am a homespun girl with a taste for culture and travel. I love walks on the beach and flower arranging. My perfect meal is home-cooked.

Occupation: Business Owner

Matches My Love Settings	....	☆☆☆☆
Matches My Distance Settings	....	☆☆
Did She Match Her Profile	....	☆☆
Did She Match Her Photos	....	☆☆
Did We Have Fun	....	☆☆
Impression of Her as a Person	....	☆☆

"The greening of Michael"

What attracted me: Her photos and our great phone calls.

I met a landscape designer from Marin. Because Marin is a wealthy area, people tend to take good care of their gardens, so business was good for the landscape design industry.

She was successful and independent. We met at a local coffee shop and decided to go to the Tiburon for dinner, overlooking the water. All night she complained about how bad her employees were and tried to get closer to me. She had a couple of glasses of wine with dinner and had loosened up a bit. After dinner, we walked to her car, where she put her hand down my pants as we kissed and asked when we could see each other again. I liked her sexual style but could not get over the constant negative things she was saying, so first impressions being what they are, I never wrote or called her again.

There was a fascinating woman I never met who lived in Novato -- just north of Mill Valley. She was exceptionally tall for a woman, and her photos were very feminine and attractive. We swapped emails and she was interested in a date. Plus, she had that surrender theme I liked and listened for -- somehow I thought she was a man, a beautiful man, but a man nonetheless, dressed as a woman. I always wondered what her voice would have sounded like. I never took the risk to find out.

WHAT'S IN A WORD ANYWAY?

UNEQUAL EXPECTATIONS

Chapter Nineteen

Swings and rings

As I mentioned before, I became interested in girls very early, and as I am telling you all about how I got to this place in my life, it seems like the right time to discuss the impact Karen Brown had on me when I was in the second grade. Now don't go to sleep on me here; this may likely be more interesting than you think.

Karen lived in a trailer park just behind a decaying market in Fir Grove, a mere walking distance from my mother's home. We both played at Aubrey Park, which had some wonderful huge swings. For several weeks I played there with her and we explored the nearby creek full of trout and crayfish. We became fast friends.

The neighborhood was full of girls, but none were more attractive than Karen. The kids there all played together, but Karen's mother was actually her grandmother, and was very strict, so anytime we stole away was that much sweeter.

After days of sneaking off we began to hold hands and even kiss. I don't know who the aggressor was, but my speculation is that we both were. Kissing more and more led to the kind of experimentation kids do. Karen was open to all kinds of touching and thus gave me my first exploration of the female anatomy.

Because of our newfound hobbies, we found some very private places to spend time in the woods behind the park, where she would instigate a session after we swung and played on the monkey bars.

One day I was passing through my mom's room and saw her jewelry box open. Inside, in plain sight, was an heirloom ring in yellow gold with onyx with a small diamond in it that looked just like what Karen should be wearing, I reasoned, so I took it.

It was one of those typical cloudy, rainy Oregon days, so Karen and I went back to our fort in the woods. The fort was constructed of some construction wood from the new school across the street -- straw, logs and branches, which offered us some shelter and kept the mud at bay.

I presented the ring to her, and she lit up like only a little girl could. We did our regular kissing and touching, and by the time she went home, she had become my official girlfriend.

By the time I got home, however, Karen's grandmother had already returned the ring and had talked to my mother, who was livid. Needless to say, I got a spanking I still remember to this day.

Afterthoughts: *"I have taken all the women I have had a long-term relationship with back to the same park where Karen Brown and I played so many years ago. I am not sure why, but it has always been charming."*

ENJOYING LIFE TOGETHER SEPARATELY

Chapter Twenty

The Redheads

Because I had broadened my search, I met three most interesting women I dubbed "The redheads": an attorney, the head of nursing for a large medical facility, and legal secretary. I have a thing for red hair, but it alone is not enough to get my attention. Red hair has an innocent quality to me, like when I watch those Celtic women sing on PBS; they look so clean and pure. Mystiques being what they are, I like it.

When Beatrice met Benedict
Age: 37
Height: 6' 0"
Body Type: Athletic
Hair Color: Red

redbirdonawire

I am well-read and well-educated, looking for an athletic, adventurous man to share travel and conversation.

Occupation: Attorney

Matches My Love Settings	....	☆☆☆☆☆
Matches My Distance Settings	....	☆☆☆
Did She Match Her Profile	....	☆☆☆☆☆
Did She Match Her Photos	....	☆☆☆☆☆
Did We Have Fun	....	☆☆☆☆☆
Impression of Her as a Person	....	☆☆☆☆☆

"Drop-dead gorgeous and smart"

What attracted me: Her photos, her positive attitude, and the fact that she loved poetry (I think).

The attorney was a Celtic Goddess: athletic, well-read (no pun intended), and wonderfully confident. We traded emails and a phone call, and I wrote a few poems for her. We both liked nature and romance and I liked a challenge, so she suggested the theme and I did my best to come up with three poems I thought she would appreciate. They got her attention and I assume made me seem different to her.

**She favors red

She favors red -- to match her blush.
I imagine her dressed in roses.
Holding her near as we dance across the plaza.
Eager for the inspiration.

She talks to cats -- they sleep on her chest.
I imagine the conversation and the answer.
Says say's "sit up here," the cat answers, "uuuummmpurrr."
Eager for the invitation.

She swims in open water
        past where the eye can see.
I imagine her gracefully gliding on the blue.
As young sea lions tickling her feet with their whiskers.
Eager for the coolness of the sea.

She is a very busy woman
        bringing order to messy lives.
I imagine her imagining the intentions of others.
She perceives, "what does that gesture mean."
Eager for the time she can favor red again.

**Thought you might like this

you're walking down a switchback trail
down down down -- towards the deep black pool
no bigger than the span of your arms in a circle
feathered clouds perch above
　　　　holding court a top the diamond peak
your eyes fill with the blackness of the mirrored image
images of sky and mountain, diamonds on black
cut only by the ever green
　　　　and woody nature of the forest
The osprey soars fishing for her young
closer and closer, down and down, bigger and bigger
and then the sun falls
　　　　behind the hills and fish boil the waters

breath in perfection - peace - damn the mosquitoes

**The Soul mate

I'll look in her eyes,
not a look for lovers but one of wonder
and if I see myself -- there inside her soul I'll anticipate

I'll compliment her smile,
not a vain compliment but a heart-felt moment
and if I see her -- there through her blush I'll know

I'll walk with her, not a walk to progress
we will move in expectation
and if I find myself -- there in her touch
She'll understand

She'll stand so still -- as I approach
our soft words spoken in quiet tones
and if her heart will race -- when we are close
She -- will -- know

We'll measure every breath every gaze
every moment we converse
all for the joy of remembering
The first kiss the first embrace
the following joy racing, exhilarating, wonder!

We met in at Starbucks near her home in the City Center on a sunny, hot Saturday morning. I arrived my usual five minutes early dressed in a blue button-down long-sleeved shirt I had selected and some really well-fitting, nice jeans. I was surprised to find her already in line when I showed up, and wow, then it hit me -- she was stunning! Tall and lean, flaming curly red hair draped across her shoulders…WOW was the only way I could describe her. I was very interested, indeed.

"Pam" I said, smiling, and reached out my hand

She smiled and blushed and I almost melted "Hi, have you ordered yet?" she asked, looking away in that nice, innocent fashion some women have. She gave me the "I like you" look and then said, "I'll wait over here," while looking down, knowing she was blushing.

I had not ordered and she was waiting for her drink, so I quickly made ordered my coffee and we sat outside in the open air. The day could not have been more perfect. The sky was clear, the temperature was agreeable, and the table was shaded. If people walked by I don't think either of us noticed. We were both a bit nervous, but that quickly faded as we began to talk. She was a little shy, I thought, for an attorney, but she soon opened up and soon we found fountains of interesting things to talk about.

I asked her about her interest in topic that we had been discussing and we began to talk about "The Burning Man," which is a ritual survival session in the desert on the hottest days of the year. Next, we drifted to the topic of swimming in open water. I recited one of the poems I wrote for her as she listened attentively and blushed; I could see she was interested and not just a little -- we really connected -- so we moved the conversation to art, culture and travel. I wanted to see if the blue-jean girl would dress for dinner, and she loved the idea.

Pam was a seasoned traveler, and we recounted our trips for what must have been an hour. I had not been to Hawaii, but she was a frequent visitor so she took me on an audio tour with her animated hand language, which illustrated her excitement. She leaned forward, began laughing and talking with her hands, and wow, when she lit up, it was amazing.

On this little virtual "tour," she snorkeled with me and did the helicopter trip as if I were right there, in her hand. I saw why she was a good attorney because she painted word pictures so well. I was reminded of her ad, which referred to "much to do about nothing." Surely she was extremely intelligent and widely read to have such a good gift of presentation.

We talked about all kinds of things after that and then took a stroll. As we continued our conversation about restaurants in the area, I fished for another date. I noticed a flower shop and asked if we could look in there. I said, "The flowers are calling to us" – very poetic, huh? I asked Pam what her favorite flower was – she looked around with some interest and then pointed at the group of fancy mums. She explained that she liked the contrast of their shapes, so I ordered a very complex bouquet for her, which I carefully designed with her consultation and my sense of romance.

With bouquet and Pam in hand, I asked her to dance once we reached the plaza. There was music playing on some speaker system that was reminiscent of an old country in Europe so I asked her to dance for the sense of adventure. She said, "Here?" I replied only with a smile and took her hand. We did a short waltz across the plaza as we said out farewells. I seemed like neither of us wanted to leave, and we kept turning back to say something the farther away we got until finally I reached the parking garage and saw her standing there waving, holding the flowers a block away.

My schedule was murder for travel, so for several weeks we IM'ed each other. I asked her out several times but she was always busy and could not meet. I tried all my IM charm, but her notes got shorter. I was sure I was being bested by some other, more interesting guy. We shared IMs and emails, but there were no follow-up dates despite my best efforts. – Ouch!

Live life to its fullest
Age: 45
Height: 5' 6"
Body Type: Average
Hair Color: Red

pamelared1

I love being outdoors as much as I like curling up in a blanket looking at the ocean, drinking wine and reading a good book.

Occupation: Executive

Matches My Love Settings	....	☆☆☆☆☆
Matches My Distance Settings	....	☆☆☆
Did She Match Her Profile	....	☆☆☆☆☆
Did She Match Her Photos	....	☆☆☆☆☆
Did We Have Fun	....	☆☆☆☆☆
Impression of Her as a Person	....	☆☆☆☆☆

"Super nice, fun to be with"

What attracted me: Her photos, her positive attitude, and our phone calls were great.

Though I continued to pine for Pam, I met another very nice woman named Teresa. Teresa was the head of nursing for a large medical facility. She and I hit it off right away, and we saw each other four or five times; we went to the theater, ballet, and Carmel for a picnic on the beach.

We met for the first time at Starbucks. The coffee date went so well, we went over to a local restaurant for sushi. The place was dimly light and lo and behold, there was another of my coffee dates, sitting in a booth with some guy. I smiled as we passed them and said hello as

Teresa and I sat three booths away, where I had a good view of my former coffee date the entire time. I never told Teresa who it was.

Teresa was the daughter of well-traveled parents who had lived overseas during most of her youth. I was very impressed by her manners and cordial nature as we talked. Our conversation went to her time in Japan, and I wondered if that culture had rubbed off on her. I had the stereotypical image that Japanese women were submissive and hoped that was not the case with Teresa.

She liked most everything I did for fun, so we made a plan and our first date was a hike and picnic. The area we live in is blessed with natural wonder, and Castle Rock is one of the most beautiful. Castle Rock is a goat trail for most people but a perfect hike if you want scenery, difficulty and a large rock to camp out on and take in the view. Anyone who can survive it is a good catch as a hiking partner. That day was extraordinarily nice. The sun was out, and it was warm and un-crowded. We found a rock overlooking a large valley and enjoyed a picnic there, resting against each other. After a single kiss we continued with our walk. She was in good shape and we did not need to rest.

The second turn was through a grove of Manzanita or Madrone trees and we stopped and embraced, celebrating the beauty of the moment against a moss-covered rock. After we kissed again in the parking lot, I was interested in more.

Our next date was dinner and theater. She invited me, so I was doubly pleased. We saw the play *Intimate Apparel* and she got great seats, paid for dinner and drove. We caught a nice meal in Mountain View at a nice sidewalk place that served California cuisine. She was beautiful as we ate, and we laughed. We concluded the evening with some passionate kissing at her doorway.

Teresa emailed me or called daily, and I suggested an outing but she countered with an invitation to dinner. I thought this was going to go well, so I went out and bought some nice wine, dressed up a little and met her at her door. I thought this was going to be a "sex date" and was excited to see how things went.

I arrived with wine, flowers and a smile. She greeted me at the door wearing a dress and an apron. With an innocent kiss, she invited me into her kitchen. I loved her hair; it was red and twisted, very natural. The food smelled good and we stood in the kitchen as she put the finishing touches on dinner. She asked me to open the wine and drank some while she finished preparing dinner. We ate formally in her dining room on nice china. We held hands while we talked, ate, and drank wine. It was very pleasant.

After dinner I helped clean up and do the dishes. Her kitchen was next to a large sliding window and we could see the exceptional number of stars that night, so we went to her back yard to stargaze and I wrapped my arms around her from behind as we leaned against the back yard brick table. I nibbled on her neck and she showed some pleasure then turned and pressed against me as we kissed. We made it to the living room and begin to become passionate, but I could sense she was not into it so after some time, I took my leave gracefully and we kissed at the door on my way out. Hmm. Not into sex, I thought?

We hiked again several times and drove down the coast, each time engaging in some passionate kissing but nothing more, so I thought this was not causing sparks in her and decided to tone down my communication to become just friendly. Maybe she just wanted to be friends, maybe she did not like sex, maybe she could not have sex. Who knows these things?

I thought that would be the end, but she kept communicating and we made another date which also ended at the door, even thought it was apparent that she had a good time.

The last date was to be the ballet. I was already seeing coffee date number 33 and we were hot for each other, but I had previously invited Teresa, so I kept my promise to her and went to dinner with her, and then to the ballet. After a wonderful date, I kissed her on the cheek at her door and said thanks for the nice date. That was the last I heard from her.

Homebody seeks some adventure
Age: 51
Height: 6' 1"
Body Type: Average
Hair Color: Red

goforitall544

I have 3 kids that are grown. I live with a dog Toto, a cat tiger and a mina bird that cannot learn its name. I work full time.

Occupation: Legal Secretary

Matches My Love Settings	....	☆☆☆☆
Matches My Distance Settings	....	☆☆☆☆☆
Did She Match Her Profile	....	☆☆☆☆☆
Did She Match Her Photos	....	☆☆☆☆☆
Did We Have Fun	....	☆☆
Impression of Her as a Person	....	☆☆☆

"Homebody"

What attracted me: She lived nearby.

Next I saw a legal secretary; our relationship consisted of many emails, some chat, several phone calls, a coffee date and a dinner out -- with no follow up. Nancy was nice enough, but a homebody and more into decorating then the outdoors, so I figured it would not work. I am surprised how fast I ruled out a relationship with her, because she was very sweet. At that time I had decided I was looking for either a very independent, outgoing woman or a surrendered one. My continued fascinations with surrender led me in interesting and dark directions.

Chapter Twenty-One

Expanding the wild world

I was really getting used to this thing. I began to look around at the more offbeat sites like Cupid, FriendFinder and True.com. I saw an ad for LavaLife on the commuter train I rode, so I investigated that. Looking at lists of dating sites was very interesting. Just try Googling "dating websites" sometime and see what happens. The truth was, I thought there was more to learn; something I had missed, and experience I wanted and made time for – I was aroused in many ways.

My best friend at the time was a co-worker. He and I spoke at length about the darker side of dating and the divisions of interests on the Internet. We reasoned over a hamburger and some wheat beer that there were just plain sex sites which must be fake, casual sex encounters sites that were beyond our experience, relationship sites where people were looking for long-term relationships, and dating sites where people wanted to make friends and have fun.

I was dying of curiosity and visited some of the more adult sites on the dark side. I'll bet that would have made for some embarrassing moments for me on a web cam as I squirmed around in my chair at work, looking at images of women baring all in ways I can only describe as "interesting." I am not a porn-monger; that stuff disgusts me, but these images were supposedly of people like me, not paid porn stars and models.

I had always been in monogamous relationships. All of my sexual experiences after 18 were with exclusive partners and I could not envision any woman I ever met doing what these women were doing – so, (gulp, squirm), I made some connections. I made a big effort to learn all I could about these supposed lifestyles. I already had a good idea what dominos were into and after the *Rocky Horror Picture Show*, I think the entire world knew about transvestites. I had played in committed relationships, even dating relationships, but this was way off the deep end even for me.

Imagine being a woman who becomes the consensual slave to a man – stop – take a deep breath -- I said imagine, remember? There were mostly men on these sites wanting to do just that for women. I reasoned, as I had already considered that kind of life, that these men could not be serious -- just remarkably horny. Yet there were so many that at least some must be from planet earth. Was there a whole parallel world out there I'd somehow missed?

And there were websites from books written by people promoting those kinds of lifestyles. I was aware of some of them. *Taken In Hand*, *Venus On Top*, *How To Spank Your Man*, and websites called Loving Domestic Discipline and Collar Me. Wow, this was the dark side for sure -- it made my mind race with questions, I found it erotic and stimulating to dig into, almost hypnotic. I had allowed myself to look deeply into a whole other world indeed.

I was soon in communication with women who got off on this lifestyle, and I was about to meet my first. I was not sure I wanted to, but I did.

Switch looking for adventure
Age: 48
Height: 5' 10"
Body Type: Few extra pounds
Hair Color: Brown

canswitchup

I am looking for a long-term subbie who wants to switch from time to time, must enjoy hard-ass play and the helplessness of bondage.

Occupation: Unknown

Matches My Love Settings	. . . .	☆
Matches My Distance Settings	. . . .	☆☆
Did She Match Her Profile	. . . .	☆☆☆☆☆
Did She Match Her Photos	. . . .	☆☆☆☆
Did We Have Fun	. . . .	☆☆
Impression of Her as a Person	. . . .	☆☆☆

"Hot and kinky – oh my God"

What attracted me: Are you kidding?

Demi was a self-proclaimed switch -- we never met for coffee, but we did meet at a Starbucks. A switch is a cross between a domino and a submissive – who knew? Demi had an image of herself in leather and she claimed to love strap-on play, which sounded very painful to me, but we hit it off. She was by day a normal, responsible woman and by night a superhero switch.

We communicated for a month before deciding to meet. she thought I was cute and said so. She wanted to show me the "scene" and I was interested, so we met in Menlo Park near a landmark we both knew at Starbucks. How ironic, I thought, this was the same Starbucks where I'd met three very nice women and passed on them -- now here I was looking into a 1960s MG approach with a woman inside.

Demi pulled over, leaned toward me and asked me my name. She handed me a hairband women wear to anchor their ponytails, elastic and fairly small then said, "Go into the bathroom, wrap this around your ____ and ____ and come back here, we are going for a ride." I went into the bathroom, thought about it, put the band on and returned as instructed.

She was a tall woman, mid-40s, and busty. By day she had said she was a professional but claimed to be going through some hard times recently. We drove out the back side of Menlo Park, up to Woodside, and to a tavern she knew. I was beginning to think I was out of my mind. I could not think of a thing to say to a woman in leather, driving a '60s MG sitting next to a man wearing a hair band around his so and so. Then the comedy of it hit me, and I began to smile and chuckle. This was adult play, just like those summers with Karen, Cathy and the Faver Twins. We were reduced to 8 years old again.

We made small talk through the drive and over drinks and then made our way back to familiar territory. I was glad to see a place I knew. It was late and the shops were closed so we sat on one of the chairs on the terraced courtyard, she put her books on my legs and said, "what in the hell are you doing? You are no submissive." I could not help but laugh. I had no answer for her. We kept in touch for several weeks after but never made another date.

ONE OF HER PETS?

Chapter Twenty-Two

Alt.com and the Slaves

Straight up – if you don't want to know about the dark side of surrender or submission, you should bypass this part of the book because I explored it with several women who sought me out from my ads on Alt.com and Yahoo.com. My meeting with Dinah made me very curious about surrender -- just what did that mean about me, I wondered? Here I was a family guy, a respected businessman and a Christian, and I was curious about what seemed to be a very dark topic.

On Yahoo I "virtually met" a woman trolling for submissive men. I asked her about her ad and she said, and I quote, "Buzz off." Not being one to take no for an answer, I pressed and asked her what she was looking for. She explained she was looking for lifestyle male – submissives to play with and take gratitude from (that is interpreted thusly: "take money for services and the men do all the work" for all you newbees). I explained my exploration into this new world, and she again said, and I quote, "Get lost."

Finally, after bugging her several more times, she sent me an invitation to join her "harem" (my words) – a three-page application which I wish I'd kept so I could have framed it. She also sent poorly worded instructions I was supposed to "obey to the letter."

I just about fell out of my chair when I opened the application form on a .doc file – careful to scan it for viruses, followed by laughter, convulsions, repulsion and deep curiosity. I thought, "Any man must be kidding, wanting to practice that." Oh my God, the application was filled with misspellings and worded so poorly, I thought, "a high school dropout wrote this, stole a photo and is trying to exploit men."

My exploration into the forbidden fruits did not mean I stopped seeing other, more conventional and independent women, but it did mean I was letting my mind wander. Registering on Alt is creepy also just because of the kinds of ads that helped support the site.

I was surprised to see several women from Match and Yahoo on the site, so I contacted them with a few questions. One was kind enough to answer. She said she did not know what kind of site it was; I thought she must be blind. The site was and is filled with sexually explicit images. I contacted about 20 women on Alt.com, but the three who contacted me on their own were the ones I actually met. These women wanted to learn about or live an alternate lifestyle where they were slaves at some level to their man. Wow, that is a mouthful. Did I just say they wanted to live as a slave to their man? I wondered just what a woman who wanted this would be like. What goes through her mind?

Ginger came from Yahoo, Lisa and Rachel from Alt. They each were really into their kinks and wanted to explore, even develop a lifestyle with someone trustworthy, who of course was me. Ginger lived a long ways away, so we did not meet until several months later. I saw Lisa first.

By this time, I was getting very good at feeling out what drove these women to want such things. There is a deeply erotic element in control and surrender. I began reading about it as much as I could and concluded that most of it on the web is to sell sex and nothing more.

The websites promoting it used models, and there were a few poorly written websites espousing real people who lived that lifestyle, but very few. The damnable thing about the web is, you never know if it is real, and websites supposedly penned by women could be written by men or, worse, by anyone who just wants to find a way to sell porn by creating erotic pictures.

One website I actually believed was a BSDM forum ("BSDM" is some silly combination of Bondage and Discipline (BD), Dominance and Submission (DS), and Sadism and Masochism (SM). They can't even get their acronyms to pan out. At any rate, I learned about people in the lifestyle, the scene and the play clubs where these people go. I had to conclude that a very small number of people actually made it a "lifestyle"; most (a very large number) practiced it in their private lives on an off-and-on basis. Okay, so real people actually do this, but what is it, and how do you live it with a woman proposing to be my slave?

Afterthoughts: *"I always felt a bit awkward on alt.com. It is not a place I can talk about openly; there are some very different habits and desires being expressed that I just do not get. I do respect people for reaching out, though."*

Looking for a master
Age: 42
Height: 5' 3"
Body Type: Few extra pounds
Hair Color: Brown

slaveforsomeone

I have some experience with the scene, and I am looking for a relationship and perhaps love with a man who knows what he wants and is going to demand it.

Occupation: Nurse

Matches My Love Settings	…………	☼
Matches My Distance Settings	…………	☼☼
Did She Match Her Profile	…………	☼☼☼☼☼
Did She Match Her Photos	…………	☼
Did We Have Fun	…………	☼☼
Impression of Her as a Person	…………	☼☼

"Intelligent woman - knows what she wants"

What attracted me: Photo of her in a corset, willingness to be real about what she wanted.

Lisa was a hospice nurse in charge of a facility in a distant yet reachable city. She was really into this kink. We swapped scenarios, stories that were extremely kinky – except hers were always more graphic then mine and very explicit. I almost broke it off before we met because I got so grossed out but I was dying of curiosity, so we met. She had concert tickets, so we arranged to meet at a local Starbucks where we would go to dinner if we liked each other and then on to the concert if all went well. I was out of my element really, thinking how I'd introduce my slave to my kids, my mother, my pastor? I arrived at Starbucks exactly at 5 p.m., and she was already there.

Lisa was a scant 5' 3" tall and a bit on the heavy side, but she dressed well and was on time. All good things for a proposed slave, I guessed. She dressed carefully after asking me what I wanted her to wear. I did not have any intensions on the date, but I am sure she thought of many alternatives until deciding on a nice dress and simple shoes. She was busty, and I liked that, but I felt like a giant next to her. I wondered what she had on under the dress but controlled my tongue and didn't ask. I had envisioned a chastity device or exotic sex toy under there, just out of sight.

We had some coffee and chatted, after which I normally would have gone home, but here was this woman who said right there that she was interested in being my slave and agreed to go to dinner with me. Stop, rewind, those ideas really don't go together do they? Well, that is what happened.

The restaurant was right next door, one of these trendy hi-tech places with a fantastic bar converted in a former garage or storefront. As we sat down, I wondered if I should order for her and asked, "Shall I order for you?" She smiled and said, "Yes, sir." That was the first time someone called me "Sir," as is so popular with the BSDM crowd. Looking at her, I thought she should be eating a small dinner salad to lose some weight, but I ordered us both the fish. We talked about her work and her day as we ate, and it was all quite normal -- except for her perfume.

By the time the concert started, her perfume was really getting to me. I could not get that smell out of my nose,

and it was overwhelming. We were in the third-row center, which, in that venue was a very good seat, but it also made escaping that much more impossible. She reached over and held my hand. She had bought the tickets to see a particular piano performer with the symphony and he was good enough, but I was getting sick from the perfume and during the intermission, we took some air.

After the concert, we drove together in my car to my house, where we had worked out a scene for the night. My apartment was about 1400 square feet and looked like most apartments. The night before she had asked me to write the scene down for her; it was kind of like role-playing but for real. In other words, she wanted me to write down what I wanted her to do.

After we were inside the door, without a word, Lisa stripped naked, took my coat and put it away then slipped off to the shower. Afterwards, she literally crawled to where I was standing, then asked for and received a series of punishments while on all fours on the carpet. Then I sat in my chair and for my entertainment, she did herself in every sense of the word in front of me while I watched. I admit it was entertaining, but I just could not get that heavy perfume smell out of my nose. Whoa.

Once again, I did not want to get involved in swapping any fluids or make any commitments, so we played "all about her," a game I invented which I assumed women had perfected so they did not have to have intercourse. She was so willing and I was so *not* willing. I tried but just could not go on. After a time I decided to drive her back to her car and the evening concluded. Ick! That smell was in my nose, my house, everywhere, literally for days!

I hated that night. She was a nice woman, responsible but just way outside my experience or desire. I sat there the next morning drinking coffee and wondered whether 6-foot goddesses like doctors or lawyers practice that. If so, it might be very interesting.

WHAT A BONDAGE DATE LOOKS LIKE.

Happy girl looking for fun guy
Age: 49
Height: 5' 11"
Body Type: Slender
Hair Color: Brown

goodcareforyou

Life is so short; I want to share it with a man who wants to live it fully. I am adventurous and quiet, jubilant and calm. I'd love to meet a man who stimulates me in every way.

Occupation: Nursing Administrator

Matches My Love Settings	....	✩✩✩
Matches My Distance Settings	....	✩
Did She Match Her Profile	....	✩✩✩✩✩
Did She Match Her Photos	....	✩✩✩✩✩
Did We Have Fun	....	✩✩
Impression of Her as a Person	....	✩✩✩✩

"Intelligent and charming - wonderful"

What attracted me: Ginger was a great woman all around -- looks, charm, smart, fun.

Ginger and I actually never met for a coffee date at an actual coffee shop; instead, she came to my house for coffee. She was from another state, so when she was visiting relatives in California, she came to my apartment. Ginger and I had been exchanging emails since near the beginning and she was a tall, good-looking professional woman who was obviously smart and interesting.

Ginger and I had similar life experiences; in fact, our upbringing sounded like we had grown up in the same neighborhood, but we had lived in different states. We were the same age and enjoyed most of the same things. She contacted me first and I would never have responded but for the little hints she included in her emails about surrender.

She asked me questions about myself and volunteered things about herself. I always enjoy a new friendship, and she was attractive. Lisa was also a breast cancer survivor, something I would not know until a month before we met. She had surgery and had gone through breast reconstruction. When she shared that I was taken aback, but then realized what I was doing and had a talk with myself. Here was a cancer survivor who wanted to be a slave. Lord knows if you survive cancer, you should surely get to do whatever you want.

Ginger and I played games online and she "obeyed" me via email. Playing was fun but tedious. She and I had talked by telephone several times before her visit. She confessed to being very aroused. Most of our conversations leading up to the meeting were about sex and arousal. That made me a little uncomfortable because we had been doing this for eight months but had really had not met yet – at least in person, and I couldn't help but remember Dinah.

A week before our meeting, she confessed that she had no feeling in the tissues of her breasts. She also said she had contracted oral and genital herpes on a romp with two men who were strangers. I told her I would never have sex with her except anally and only then with a condom if we ever had such a relationship. She made a case for all the different kinds of protection one can use nowadays and how she was an expert on this, being in medicine. I said no, no, no.

Nevertheless, she persisted and we met on a cold night in December at my apartment. In person, Ginger was impressive. She had a nice confidence to her; she exuded professionalism. She was tall, busty, and slender. That plus the intelligence proved a powerful attraction for me, and I invited her in to the living room. My living space was well-decorated and had a chair set a few feet from the loveseat, where I asked her to sit. As we made small talk about her trip and I put her coat away, I made coffee for us. She wore a tight sweater and pants; unfair, I thought. My horns were coming up as I sat in my chair near her.

She turned the conversation to surrender again, but I was past the point of playing games and said, "Stand up, go into the bathroom, strip, take a shower, and come out her in nothing but a towel." She did exactly what I said, so when she came out, I spoke in a commanding tone, "Give me the towel" and she did. There she was, standing in front of me naked, still looking very confident. We played "Do what I say" and talked for more than an hour. I got to see her closely. It was the first time I had seen reconstructive surgery, and it was not bad, but I was destined to never have sex with her even though she was a most attractive woman.

I asked her to put her clothes on, we finished our coffee, and I walked her to her car.

I am not a monster. I could not live with the thought of a woman looking for connection because she felt so low about herself that she wanted to be a slave because she had no other options. Clearly Ginger had some emotional trauma, destruction of her self-worth or self-confidence from the cancer, the surgery. I pinged Lisa and sure enough, she had some destruction in her past as well. This made me feel very low. I reminded myself that these were intelligent women, especially Ginger, so if they want that and I want that, it should be up to us, right? I really never did work it out in my mind except to take a mental note about the sense of self-destruction.

Afterthoughts: *"I pondered the question many times, 'Why is it that I never accepted the offers for control over sex? I think there are two reasons. I felt it was too much work to control another, and I could never explain it to my children without blushing."*

"I don't think for a moment that every women who wants to be submissive is actually so. Most everyone has an agenda. Most everyone has desires and we all seem to attempt to make them happen."

Interested to learn more
Age: 41
Height: 5' 6"
Body Type: Slender
Hair Color: Black

comeflywithme

I have almost no experience with this. I am looking for a nice man who wants to walk me through submission. It turns me on.

Occupation: Stewardess

Matches My Love Settings	....	☼☼
Matches My Distance Settings	....	☼
Did She Match Her Profile	....	☼☼☼☼☼
Did She Match Her Photos	....	☼☼☼☼☼
Did We Have Fun	....	☼☼☼
Impression of Her as a Person	....	☼☼☼

"If you see me, run – very fast"

What attracted me: Her photos, and the fact that she contacted me.

Rachel was a flight attendant from the old school, you know, a flight attendant! Big-teeth smile, beautiful and petite. She was compulsive about learning about surrender and just experimenting with it, so I was careful to ask about destruction in advance, and she had none.

Rachel was one of those bolder women who contacted me towards the end of my search. We met at my place, then walked to Starbucks through the late autumn air. It was around 4 p.m. and we talked about all the trees changing color. Her smile would ring a bell, I noted.

After coffee we took off for dinner at a local haunt and I watched her eat like a bird as I enjoyed a steak. She was graceful, 5'5" and had not an ounce of fat showing anywhere. I am a good student of body language, and she was very over-aroused and nervous. She had just met a man (that would be me) from the Internet who knew some intimate secrets about her, and she was really turned on. Rachel had a different language about surrender: she called it "submissive," but I knew from experience that submissive people don't often do assertive things like she was doing. I thought she was going to burst right there in the restaurant, watching her blush as she squirmed on the bench.

We walked back slowly and she moved very close to me and wrapped herself around me, which I took as a signal to proceed "full steam ahead." Back at my place I turned up the apartment temperature, took her coat and we sat together. We began kissing passionately and she moved onto my lap in seconds. I moved us to the floor where she straddled me, so we were as close as two people can be with their clothes on.

I noticed she was getting shy when I unbuttoned her blouse and she slowed me down but did not stop as she gulped some words out through her arousal, "My breasts are very small, but don't worry, I am having a boob job in LA next week." That is exactly what she said, word for word.

I should have laughed, I should have seen that as a clue to stop myself but she took both my hands under her open shirt and began kissing me again passionately. I stood up and picked her up, which took some effort, and we danced for a long time with me telling her what to do and her doing it; this was a good time for us both. She was so excited.

She was naked while we danced and I had all my clothes on. I took her to the shower and washed her all over, then put her on the bed and gave her a massage from heaven; she burst out on sounds of joy five times to my magic fingers, which I skillfully used to her advantage.

I avoided intercourse and oral sex with her because I did not want the gift that keeps on giving and we did not have an exclusive relationship. After her climaxes a grim look came over her face and she said and I quote, "There is no love," I said, "Excuse me?" She whimpered, "There is no love, this is empty." She lay there looking puzzled, then bounced up and put her clothes up to herself like I was not supposed to see her naked, then proceeded to get dressed, all the while apologizing, saying, "I have to go now." She hurried to get her things and left. About two minutes after she left, my phone rang. She had forgotten some article of clothing and wanted me to bring it out. Wow, that did not turn out like I thought it would. That was the first woman who climaxed five times and did not like it.

I took a glass, filled it with amaretto, collapsed in my chair and watched football.

Chapter Twenty-Three

More words about words

In my encounters with women online, I began to accept that there were differences of opinion about what the basic descriptions of words meant. When it comes to hair color, just forget it. Women change their hair color, so it really does not matter too much if they say blond, brunette or red because tomorrow they might be something different.

Age is a thing, I think, that has some mystique. When my mom became 29 for the 29th continual year, I realized that age was an interesting social phenomenon with older women. So when she says 47 and she is 57, what am I supposed to think? It is a lie but seems to be one of those socially acceptable ones that levels the playing field. Most women assume that men won't date someone older than they are.

The one that got me the most was the infamous "a few extra pounds." So a few is like one or two of three, right? Or perhaps a few means some small percentage. Or it might mean, "I used to be a few pounds lighter." So if your ideal body weight is 130 and you are in the range of normal, say 120-140 then you are likely "average," right? Perhaps 141,142 or 143 would be a few extra pounds? Perhaps they needed another category called "obviously fat."

If seems like we have euphemisms for all kinds of things that we find difficult to accept, like going bald is now "hair loss" or "thinning hair." People who are fat have "a few extra pounds." Great big women use acronyms like "BBW" which means "Big Beautiful Woman." One woman had a rant on her ad about men who were fat, saying something like "If you have a few extra pounds listed, it had better be a few, because anything more that 9 percent over your weight class means you are definitely fat!"

If we are all trying to be polite or politically correct, how, then, will we ever know if we are speaking the same language? Then there was the question of whether people actually see themselves in that light.

As I mentioned earlier, my first foray into the Internet dating scene was very early on. In the early days of the Internet, all the daters used bulletin boards. I met one woman who said she was "thick" and "big boned," and when it came time to meet, she said we should go dancing and that she actually weighed 300 pounds, but not to worry, she knew how to dress... Well, to me, that is going overboard and just a lie. Maybe she lied to herself, maybe she just lied to me, but it is still a lie.

So the question is when is something a lie? And when is it a little white lie? If I were to find a trusting relationship, surely it should not be built on a lie. What is the true definition of a word or phrase? Was it safe to build a trusting relationship on a polite expression or an interesting way of looking at a word? I decided to overlook age and hair color, but it had better not go further than that.

THE FASHION OF IDEOLOGICAL DIFFERENCES

Chapter Twenty-Four

Cleaning it all up

I began talking to guy friends and even some of the women I met online about various aspects of my experiences. I realized just how much variety I had experienced in such a short time. I really could not take it all in. One co-worker suggested I develop the kind of plan I would make for a multimillion-dollar project, suggesting that the time I took to do it would be the price of a divorce. So I reformulated my ads once again.

Ad 1: *Eclectic and Adventurous????*

This is me: I have an edge, am very active, eclectic and adventurous. I am almost always happy, ride the shopping cart in the lot at Costco, love to play and flirt. Hiking, exploring, the arts, architecture, mountain streams, the beach, fine restaurants, bookstores, high tech and high tea all in the same week - that's me. I am the kind of friend you'd want in troubled times. I am fit in every way. I know myself very well. I am kind to everyone, almost never argue, listen well, read body language, read poetry.

If you met me you'd find me confident, bright, emotionally available, affectionate, progressive, and interesting.

I am looking for a woman who loves romance: such as dancing in the open air or sharing a blanket at the beach watching the sea birds play. You'd love being in nature and in the city. Love art and theater, intellectual and cultural topics, book stores, coffee shops, gardens. You'd be kind, generous and loyal; full of life, blush easily and be able to take risks with your heart; well-spoken and read; witty, smart, and adventurous.

There is no magic formula but I'd like you to be tall, fit, smile and laugh at the drop of a hat, engaging in conversation, independent, have an edge. It'd be great if you were professional or in management/leadership.

I am open to ideas.

Ad 2: *Imagine sipping coffee and talking about things of the day, walking around the lake having a chit chat, exploring a gallery - a garden or a misty riverside, or a meal and conversation watching people pass by - that is what I am looking for. Who I am looking for: a friend. I am open to a LTR but based on a solid friendship.*

I prize beauty for sure, but a deep, intelligent, caring and resourceful woman gets not only my attention, but my complete respect as well.

I am drawn to confidence; I know everyone is a little shy -- even the most confident people. The woman I am looking for is likely successful in many areas of her life. I am not intimidated by success, I find it very attractive. Success does not have to be money, "cuz money can't buy you love" - Beatles

If you are shy, easily wounded, withdrawn, or prone to possessiveness, I am not your guy. I prize a good mixture of reason and emotions, zeal and peace. Everyone likes to get crazy sometimes.

A little about me:

I am a good man, but not a simple one. I am easy, expressive, can tell you how I feel, and what I am thinking, I have a pretty good idea of what I want from life, yet remain flexible.

I am reserved but not shy, confident but not imposing, a natural leader and a good follower. I listen well, am emotionally available. I love to explore and learn. I am affectionate; know the art of touch and anticipation and can be a gentleman if a woman wants to be treated like a lady.

I work as a technologist, leading a large business unit. I like one on one and small group communication best, but am quite comfortable leading conferences and teaching seminars.

I take care of myself, run, walk, lift, crunches, etc..., eat well, and live an active life. I travel, browse shops and galleries, enjoy fine and simple dining, camp, fish, hike, and generally enjoy life indoors and out.

Notes to the chef:

I don't have the wherewithal or energy to chase all the time, so you do a little, I'll do a little and we'll see how it goes. Besides - isn't that how friendships work?

If you have questions or flags about my bio, please don't hesitate to ask. Life is an adventure, let's get going together.

Ad 3: *Looking for someone different????*

This is me: kind to everyone, almost never argues, listens well, reads body language, reads poetry. I am almost always happy, sometimes bound up several steps just because, ride the shopping cart in the lot at Costco, love to play and flirt with my someone special, believe in true love, remember things about you.

I am a man's man, like to sweat during exercise, exercise until it hurts, get off on helping others become successful. I compliment frequently/easily; write poetry and sing to those whose heart is moved by such things. I am playful and witty, it is just in me.

I cannot, by my very core being, be disingenuous in a relationship; if I am being romantic it is because I feel that way about you. Never cheated, believe in telling things straight up (buffered to your mood), find it wonderful to get to know someone.

I am sometimes reserved but never shy, confident, a natural leader and a good follower. I am emotionally available. I love to explore and learn. I am affectionate; know the art of touch and anticipation; can be a gentleman if a woman wants to be treated like a lady. I am progressive, dependable, a good friend for troubled times.

I believe in "soul mates," I think soul mates must be forgiving by nature, think the best of others, have a strong connection together, and otherwise just be nice people. Mine would love romance, would love the thought of dancing in the open air; be kind, generous and loyal; full of life, blush easily and be able to take risks with her heart; well-spoken and read; witty, smart, adventurous.

There is no magic formula for who I am looking for. I'd like you to be tall, smile and laugh at the drop of a hat, engaging, independent. Dating is nice - let's just have fun; relationships are nicer - let's get to know each other and share special moments.

I have eclectic tastes in activities; I just like lots of different things both indoors and out. Love most everything, especially a nice meal or cup of coffee and conversation.

After cleaning up my ads, I put aside my curiosities and got back to who I was really looking for. My ads turned up lots of leads.

Back to the real world

Tech meets redwoods
Age: 42
Height: 5' 9"
Body Type: Slender
Hair Color: Red

naturalgeekgirl

My job keeps me very busy and in my spare time, I love to hike and explore small towns. I want a man who is gentle and intelligent, sensual and intellectual.

Occupation: Technical Manager

Matches My Love Settings	....	☆☆☆
Matches My Distance Settings	....	☆☆☆
Did She Match Her Profile	....	☆☆☆☆☆
Did She Match Her Photos	....	☆☆☆☆☆
Did We Have Fun	....	☆☆☆☆☆
Impression of Her as a Person	....	☆☆☆☆☆

"Very nice woman"

What attracted me: Her photos, her positive attitude, we were both in tech.

Emma was a technical manager and a self-proclaimed follower of Wicca. I did not know what Wicca was, so I looked at some websites to learn more. She was a witch, a dyed-in-the-wool witch – who knew they were real? Not a broom-riding, crooked black hat, wart on her nose witch; but a gorgeous redhead who could talk tech witch. Okay, I know, what in the world was I doing going out with a witch? I was curious just what a witch was. Truthfully I did not know they even existed, I had just heard rumors. Really, though, I am open-minded and even once went to an Episcopal church on a dare, so why not!

We met for coffee in Emeryville to see if we wanted to go out. She and I had "our trade" in common and as we had exchanged emails we both got interested so we arranged the date at Skates on the Bay after coffee if it worked out. She was stunning. We greeted each other with a formal, European kiss that I enjoyed. We walked around the open entrance of Skates while we waited to be seated, talking about her work. We were seated on the waterside of the restaurant, but I never looked at the bay or the view – I was looking at her. We shared war stories (work talk) while having soft drinks.

Dinner came before I asked her about Wicca. She was just experimenting with it, she said. What a letdown that was. I was sure I was going to hear about naked rituals and dances around fires. She said she was attending some kind of Wiccan church and suggested I look at their website. Well, that was interesting but unsatisfying; I think I liked my visions of naked rituals better.

Skates restaurant is on the Berkeley marina that overlooks San Francisco Bay, the bridges and the city itself. That night was exceptionally beautiful. There was very little wind, cool temperatures (that means no fog) and clear skies. The lights flickered on the water and the moon smiled down on us. After dinner we walked around the marina at her insistence. It was cold and she wanted my arm around her and gave clues I understood without having to ask. As we walked and I held her up against me, we talked about past relationships, which is not a good primer for a first date.

She told me the story of her most recent relationship. It was a relationship that had ended badly -- she was hurt and wanted to take things slowly. They had lived together and the breakup left her feeling empty. I am not a "take things slowly" kind of guy, as you may have gathered by now, so it was disappointing to listen to, but I listened with empathy, asking questions from time to time.

When our date was ending, she asked me to walk her to her car. At the car she unbuttoned my coat, smiling and giggling while she did it, opened her coat, revealing the nice dress she had worn to dinner and took my arms inside around her and pressed up against my chest and laid against my chest pressed against her car while we kissed passionately. We were both warm and comfortable and doing what grown-ups do. Swing, she was making sure I remembered her, I thought in hindsight, and I did but never made a follow-up date with her because of her former "take it slow" statement.

2 tickets to paradise, join me?
Age: 50
Height: 5' 6"
Body Type: Slender
Hair Color: Blown

saclookingformore

Hi there! Thanks for taking the time to look at my profile. I'm a kind, very affectionate, friendly, and independent woman who would like to find the same in a man.

Occupation: Project Manager

Matches My Love Settings	....	☼☼☼☼
Matches My Distance Settings	....	☼
Did She Match Her Profile	....	☼
Did She Match Her Photos	....	☼☼
Did We Have Fun	....	☼☼
Impression of Her as a Person	....	☼

"Avoid at all costs"

What attracted me: Photo of her as a dominatrix for Halloween – I thought she might be adventurous.

This woman, who, for lack of other credentials, I suppose, represented herself as a project manager. She had a photo of herself in a dominatrix outfit in her profile, which got my attention. We did nothing more than exchange emails and meet for coffee halfway between us (35 miles or so one way). Why I met with her, I don't know for sure. She was too far away, she was rough, and she did not like the outdoors.

Life's an adventure, let's go for it
Age: 47
Height: 5' 9"
Body Type: Average
Hair Color: Blown

realpropgirl09

I love the city, its restaurants, culture and people. I also love driving through wine country and up to the coast at Mendocino.

Occupation: Real Estate Agent

Matches My Love Settings	....	☆☆☆☆
Matches My Distance Settings	....	☆☆
Did She Match Her Profile	....	☆☆☆☆☆
Did She Match Her Photos	....	☆☆☆☆☆
Did We Have Fun	....	☆
Impression of Her as a Person	....	☆☆

"Gossip-monger"

What attracted me: Her photos.

My next adventure was with a realtor in San Francisco; she, like all those in her trade, was friendly, so we met at Starbucks in Levi Plaza and decided to go to an early dinner next door at the Italian restaurant. There is a flower shop there, so I picked a really nice rose for her while we walked by. I carried the flower and her hand to the restaurant, where we ate and talked. This woman was in love with gossip and pressed me for every story, and as you can tell, I have a few. I grew tired of the one-way dialogue, told her that I had let my meter running out (which was true) and excused myself, paid the check. Next! BYW I got a 45 parking ticket too.

I Work Hard and Play Harder
Age: 47
Height: 6' 2"
Body Type: Few extra pounds
Hair Color: Blown

rhapsodyinblack

I am back here after being in the east for some time. I love this town and am looking for a nice man to spend some quality time with.

Occupation: Attorney

Matches My Love Settings	....	☆☆☆☆☆
Matches My Distance Settings	....	☆☆
Did She Match Her Profile	....	☆☆☆☆
Did She Match Her Photos	....	-
Did We Have Fun	....	☆☆
Impression of Her as a Person	....	☆☆☆☆☆

"Extremely nice woman"

What attracted me: We connected on the telephone.

Some women are very good with their photos. One trick I learned from a woman in the South Bay was that black clothes against a black background hide a multitude of pounds. Before you think me a true monster, you should realize a few pounds is no big deal and some pounds is cool, too, if we have chemistry but, and I use that term with meaning, complete exaggeration does not do much towards building a relationship of trust.

We met at a local coffee house in a quaint little town in the Santa Cruz foothills on a brilliant sunny Saturday morning. I got a wire chair table outside adjacent to the park and waited for her. I saw her from a distance walking toward me. At first glance I could see she was almost as tall as I was and much wider. This woman was warm, wonderful and very wide. She took up two seats. We drank coffee as I pondered what to do. I don't tell lies, so I decided to remain silent. After coffee we walked around the quaint town as she gave me the nickel tour.

Most of the quant town was close to the freeway, something one does not notice until walking about and it becomes difficult to hear because of the roaring of the cars whizzing by behind the oleander and trees. We made a loop together and at the end, she kissed me straight up and asked when we would see each other again. I made a gesture, something like a shrug and a smile and she added, "Is there any chance?" I said, "I don't think so," then went on my way to the car. I felt sad for her because she was such a nice woman.

Fun Girl Looking for Fun Guy
Age: 54
Height: 5' 4"
Body Type: Average
Hair Color: Black

lovelylakegirl

I have been alone for a couple of years and am now looking for the right man to spend time with, someone who is successful, knows how to get things done and wants more in life.

Occupation: Real Estate Agent

Matches My Love Settings	....	☆
Matches My Distance Settings	....	☆☆☆☆☆
Did She Match Her Profile	....	☆
Did She Match Her Photos	....	☆
Did We Have Fun	....	☆
Impression of Her as a Person	....	☆☆

"Needs an older gent"

What attracted me: Courtesy date; she was my neighbor.

A woman contacted me who lived in my neighborhood. She was a realtor, Chinese and eight years my senior. I agreed to meet her because she was my neighbor, so we met at the local Border's Book Store after finding that Peets was closed. That Borders had a Seattle's Best coffee shop in it. Wyn was a semi-successful realtor who borrows her friend's Mercedes when trying to impress people – enough said? We talked for a few minutes and then parted both the wiser. She paid for the coffee.

Afterthoughts: *"eharmony leaves off the photos and the bios until the end of their process, which makes me uncomfortable at best because so many times the person does not live up to their rhetoric."*

TRUTH IN ADVERTISING

Chapter Twenty-Five

Two pains and a train wreck

Okay, this has nothing to do with coffee dates but it's interesting. This is the kind of information you cannot find or pay for. I was tempted to use their real names, but virtue got the better of me so you will just have to wonder.

Linda was a broadcaster who also loved to swim. We both had ads on several well-known dating sites and I contacted her with a few questions about her ad. She was a babe, blond and well-toned. We exchanged emails for a time, then talked on the phone. We both worked in San Francisco, so she kept pressing me to meet, which I was not ready for because I was traveling so much. During one of our conversations I mentioned I swam sidestroke most often when doing laps (keeps the water out of my ears). She laughed and said, "You're no swimmer at all. Real swimmers would laugh you out of the pool." Well – she is likely right that real swimmers with a lot of time on their hands might think me odd, but what are you gonna do – stop swimming because someone does not like how you do it?

I was really busy still, but she kept pressing, claiming I must be a fraud because I would not meet her. Finally, she sent me a very nasty email saying everything I said was a lie, I was a fraud and she was going to turn me in to the authorities. I pondered this for a while and thought, "Who does she mean? The dating police?" This woman had all the looks a woman can have and the social graces of Attila the Hun. I can't imagine a long-term relationship with such a woman! Ouch!

Molly, "the train wreck," found me on Yahoo and introduced herself as "My Julia Roberts" and I was her "Richard Gere." That was creepy and an obvious reference to the movie *Pretty Woman*, in which Gere is a successful businessman who needs an escort, and Roberts plays that escort. They fall in love and he saves her from a life of prostitution.

Molly was very wordy in her emails, something I was used to when women had lots of questions, but not when they were sharing about "our" future. She made offers of "taking care of me" (a sexual reference). I was kind and explained that we both have no connection to either character in the movie as I was in tech and she was on welfare and a single mother and I was not looking to "be taken care of."

Molly was devastatingly cute, 5' 7" straight hair, slender, great smile, nice-looking. After a half-dozen emails where she started asking for a ticket to come out to see me so we could fall in love (she lived in a faraway Canadian Province), I told her I was absolutely not interested and gave her some advice about men. I analyzed her ad for her at her request and suggested some changes to help her meet the man of her dreams.

Molly was religious and "destined" to find a man because she was praying and her faith was driving her convictions. I suggested she reword her ad to describe her actual situation, how she feels about God telling her what to do, and what she wants. Then I told her she shouldn't use movie illustrations when contacting men, that man just want it straight up. She did so and contacted me after each of the men responded to her – she got a lot of responses, too. There was a silence of several weeks and I thought she was off to her next victim. Then bang, she wrote again and sent photos of her wedding. Oh my God, I thought, she got married after two weeks. The guy had flown up to Northern Canada in his private plane and the two had married somehow – is that even possible, I wondered? I supposed so, so I congratulated her and wished her the best.

Several months went by and she contacted me again, this time with more photos of her dressed up. She asked if we were still a happening thing and made offers to meet up and "take care of me." This time she used more suggestive words about giving me everything I could want. I replied with questions about her marriage. "Molly, what happened to your husband?" She responded that her guy had left her, that they were not "legally" married, but in God's eyes they were. She continued that she had become pregnant and lost the child and not to worry, all was well. Oh, my, I thought, twirled around in my chair a few times, took a deep breath and thanked God that I did not get involved with her. I felt for her but did not respond as it would only encourage her, and she needed to be as far from me as she could get. Thank God for Northern Canada.

One other woman who was very interesting was Mandy. Mandy was an executive for a popular website. We met on Match.com, exchanged a few emails and a telephone call, and then decided not to meet. Then when she appeared again in my "best fits" bin because she had taken a personality profile that almost matched mine, I decided to contact her again. Mandy and I chatted for some time on the telephone and planned a coffee date together. She was coming back from a road trip, so we made a date near her home for that Wednesday night. I write poetry often just for the hell of it, but I decided to prime the pump a little and sent her a nice note and told her I would send along a poem.

Sunday I sent the poem, which was romantic and artsy (I was feeling creative). We were exchanging about three emails a day at that time, so I was not surprised to see her name in my in box. She blasted me with a three-paragraph manifesto about why that was so inappropriate. She explained that we hardly knew each other and that was so overboard -- how could I ever consider doing that for a perfect stranger, and further, to not contact her again. Well, I guess that was that -- she must have had a bad day. I never knew poems could cause such a response; childish, romantic, dumb, hokey maybe, but not consternation.

Afterthoughts: *"I have accepted that there are things no one can reason their way through. I think love, hope, joy, admiration, peace and beauty need no logic."*

"The truth was I needed to like their photos to trust the women I met and when their photos did not portray them I did not trust them."

Chapter Twenty-Six

The pre-food groups

A couple of the women I dated suggested I put this in the book because they found it helpful and interesting. Part of my search was the thinking process I used to filter in or out who I thought I was looking for. It went beyond the criteria of what a woman liked to do in her spare time and leaned towards how she thought and behaved in life, even beyond what she might be looking for.

I reasoned that it boils down to two parts. The first part is the most important -- understanding the decision-making processes of women about love relationships and sustaining long-term relationships. The second part is about what people can and cannot negotiate in a love or long-term relationship.

No matter how hardened my logic is, I must admit that matters of the heart are beyond understanding; I just don't have that much energy to spend on understanding. I want things to be as simple and straightforward as possible. I believe in soul mates because I've seen them together; I believe in bad relationships because I've been in them; and I believe in applying my best efforts in getting to know any woman I am considering a long-term love relationship with.

The food groups come out of my understanding that at some point I will be in a good relationship because I will find a woman who benefits as much from me being me as I do from her being her, a match made in heaven. However, you get to look into other relationships until you find one.

The more important part is understanding how people, and, in this case, women think. I found that women tended to fall into certain "camps" in their outlook in developing relationships with men. These camps describe a woman's decision-making process pretty well.

One example is a woman who believes in destiny. I do jump in the water with both feet, but I don't throw caution to the wind. Being a planner for a living affords me to move fast while making the best decisions; this allows me to see how things go while I'm experimenting. Being secure about myself and having a good self-image allows me to take lumps in stride without taking them personally. None of those things adds up to destiny.

To find a woman who is like me, I found it necessary to open up, make myself vulnerable, and tell the women I was meeting who I was and what I wanted in life. That sounds logical right up until chemistry comes into play. Let's say I met a woman who was a lot like me, we hit it off, and then when we meet, one or the other doesn't have chemistry. That makes me admit that you can't rely on logic alone. I admit it, okay? Chemistry is nine-tenths of the law and nothing I can do can change that. So being able to separate those women with whom I have better chemistry is the winning formula. I just have to be able to know the name of their particular "camp" so I can find them!

Chapter Twenty-Seven

Mind melds and no coffee

I had some wonderful connections with women I never met. Well, that is to say, most of my connections I would never meet in person, but there were a few exceptional ones who helped me learn about myself, communication and more about what women want.

Deanna and I clicked right away but because of our schedules, we could never seem to find a time to meet. She was in sales, traveling extensively, and I was traveling to Chicago and San Diego rather often. She had a way of turning what I had written into something else, so we spent lots of time explaining what we meant and asking questions.

Deanna was attracted to me because she saw me as a "wild child" and she liked "non-traditional" relationships. I told her that I did not put much into gender roles and she countered that she thought that was great and looked forward to an "unconventional relationship." I responded that I did not think it was unconventional for a couple to choose the roles they would take in a relationship. She volleyed back with, "I appreciate that you appreciate the leadership of a woman."

That went on and on until she just stopped writing. I pinged her and she said she thought I was looking for a strange relationship, so she was no longer interested. Well, the lesson learned here is that words do have meanings, and some words trigger big responses.

Lynn was an exercise nut and she got offended that I was not more supportive of her exercise. We had been communicating for a week or so and were almost to the "let's get coffee" phase when she sent me an FU email. It appears she interpreted something I said to mean that I thought she was not attractive. I scanned my email over and over and could not find a thing intimating that.

One woman I wrote to I thought I saw on another site with a different name. I said, "Hey, I know you from Match, we should get together because our personality profiles line up so well." She wrote back and said, "That sounds interesting but I am not on Match.com." Ooops. I looked and sure enough, they could have been twins, so I asked if she had a twin. She wrote back to tell me to stop communicating with her because she thought I was nut.

I was contacted by a woman on Yahoo who said she found my ad intriguing, so we communicated for a while. After some time, she asked me out and I said, "I don't think so." When she asked why, I told her I did not have a strong attraction to her photos. She countered that she looked better in person. I said, "That may very well be, but we still need an attraction to decide to get to the date, right?" She said I was shallow.

So, suffice it to say, I did not always have positive communications, and I wrote some things that offended some of my prospects.

Chapter Twenty-Eight

Very nice people

Not everyone you meet online is a train wreck, sex slave or Celtic goddess; there are some very nice women who are just normal, nice people out there. They come from many different careers. One owned her own business, one was a corporate merger specialist, one woman was a medical specialist, and another a musician.

Making music of life together
Age: 46
Height: 5' 9"
Body Type: Few extra pounds
Hair Color: Brown

stringsandthings

I'd love to be doing music full-time but I still have to work to finance it. Plus points if you can tine a guitar. Let's get together and make some music.

Occupation: Varied

Matches My Love Settings	....	☆☆☆
Matches My Distance Settings	....	☆☆☆☆
Did She Match Her Profile	....	☆☆☆
Did She Match Her Photos	....	☆
Did We Have Fun	....	☆
Impression of Her as a Person	....	☆☆

"Nice woman – sweet voice"

What attracted me: Her music.

Linda lived in a nice part of the Bay Area. She worked during the day at something akin to play and did her music the rest of the time. She played small venues by herself and entertained the crowd with her own, very unique style of music. We spoke over the phone and met for coffee. She was a nice woman who was having many issues with her health at the time. We had dinner at a restaurant near my home with intelligent conversation and laughter; musicians are great to talk to. After the meal we went to the lake near my apartment and walked a bit -- she was suffering from foot and hip issues so she could only walk a few feet. She would make a good friend, but I am an active guy and I'd be doing activities alone – sad.

Looking for a man interested in mergers
Age: 42
Height: 5' 10"
Body Type: Average
Hair Color: Brown

jennifer007

I work hard and still find time to play. By background is in business and I relocated to the Bay Area after a successful merger to get back to my roots.

Occupation: Executive

Matches My Love Settings	....	☆☆☆☆☆
Matches My Distance Settings	....	☆☆☆
Did She Match Her Profile	....	☆☆☆☆☆
Did She Match Her Photos	....	☆☆☆☆☆
Did We Have Fun	....	☆☆☆☆☆
Impression of Her as a Person	....	☆☆☆☆☆

"I made a mistake– she was great"

What attracted me: Her photos, her positive attitude, and our phone calls were great.

Jenny was an executive and part of a corporate merger specialty team for a large financial firm. We met at Starbucks near her home, and she was sweet and comfortable so we decided to push the envelope and do a date in Carmel as it's very nice in autumn there and was a pleasant day.

I packed a few picnic items and we met up in front of Peets Coffee. It was nice of her to drive down, saving me an hour-round trip to pick her up. Our drive down to Carmel was wonderful, with lots of light conversation and laughing. The day was sunny, the sky was bluest blue and all was sweet. My habit in Carmel was to stop for breakfast at the Benedict Café, so we did. She was the perfect companion: polite, participatory and well mannered.

We strolled through the galleries, held hands, shared an occasional embrace, told art stories, sipped coffee and ate some chocolate. Then when we could walk no more we went down to the city beach. The air was cold that day, so I came prepared with a tarp, blankets, and several pillows along with the picnic goodies. We watched the birds fish and the children run. I held her as we shared our life stories and dreams. For dinner we went back up to Monterey to the Chart House restaurant, which overlooks the water where the otters play – another perfect event.

Driving home, I sang songs and we laughed. I walked her to her car back at Peets, we kissed several times and she said, "Let's do this again." I smiled and said, "You are a most charming companion."

We never made arrangements for another date. I had never before or since met such a charming and perfect date. They should make Jenny into ingredients for harmony. Something in my gut told me I needed to protect her from me because she was too perfect for words, so I never pursued that relationship.

Afterthoughts: *"My God, I met such a nice woman. I am better for our meeting. I especially enjoyed singing in the car on the way back from Carmel in duet."*

"Of the many women I met, only a few enjoyed poetry. I was confused by this until I came to realize that it is about the words, not their organization."

Active and restful, let's connect
Age: 45
Height: 5' 9"
Body Type: Slender
Hair Color: Brown

trikeandbike

I am active and want a man friend who is, too. I love all sports, even love watching them. I am also a cultured girl who loves the theater and fine wine. Can you keep up?

Occupation: Business Owner

Matches My Love Settings	....	☆☆☆☆☆
Matches My Distance Settings	....	☆☆☆
Did She Match Her Profile	....	☆☆☆☆☆
Did She Match Her Photos	....	☆☆☆☆☆
Did We Have Fun	....	☆☆☆☆☆
Impression of Her as a Person	....	☆☆☆☆☆

"Great catch -- she was not interested in me"

What attracted me: Her photos, her positive attitude, and our phone calls were great.

Catherine was a successful businesswoman who ran a company with lots of employees in a nearby area. She was an avid exercise nut, an attribute that I liked very much about her. Her form of exercise, however, was not like mine, but we overlooked that after emails and phone calls and met up at a Starbucks in her town. She was a bicycler, and those who do this seem to be in a type of cult – she wheeled 30 to 50 miles a day. She was tall and slender, smart as a whip and extremely nice. We both felt good at the meeting but never went forward to schedule a date – my loss; she was a very good catch.

Have critters? Want a few?
Age: 44
Height: 5' 10"
Body Type: Slender
Hair Color: Brown

cynthiana

I love my life, I love nature and animals, I love exploring. So where oh where is a man who loves them too?

Occupation: Business Owner

Matches My Love Settings	....	☆☆☆☆☆
Matches My Distance Settings	....	☆☆☆
Did She Match Her Profile	....	☆☆☆☆☆
Did She Match Her Photos	....	☆☆☆☆☆
Did We Have Fun	....	☆☆☆☆☆
Impression of Her as a Person	....	☆☆☆☆☆

"Great catch for someone interested in animals"

What attracted me: Her photos, her positive attitude, and our phone calls were great.

Cindy was a charming woman who lived in a quant town with adorable animals – the perfect life. She had just gotten out of a short long-distance relationship and decided not to date anyone unless they lived closer to her -- and I unfortunately did not. Yet she invited me up for coffee anyway. After coffee we planned a hike date, so we met on Saturday morning and walked around a local lake laughing and making small talk. We had a great time looking at the water and birds as we strolled, occasionally bumping and touching. After the walk we did not want our date to end so we both began to invent reasons to continue. Lunch was suggested even though it was only 11 a.m. We ate at a sidewalk café on a business central street, taking in the sun and enjoying each other. I reached across the table to hold her hand, which she eagerly opened. We had a great morning and parted with a kiss around 1 p.m. Then she sent an email followed by a call, saying I lived too far away – so sad.

Afterthoughts: *"I decided that I was a good catch and thought I needed a relationship where I was as much a benefit to a woman as she was to me."*

Chapter Twenty-Nine

Oh where, oh where, can you be?

By this point, I was getting tired of dating and decide to greatly restrict my ads and the websites on which I was currently active. I reformulated my ad and limited myself to eHarmony.com, PerfectMatch.com and Match.com. I created a list of must-haves (very important), and like-to-haves so I could see plainly who to date. I created some canned responses from my previous emails and set out again. I no longer considered photos in my initial contact because most of them did not look like the women I would ultimately meet anyway.

Ad: **Who I am:

I am interesting to talk to, don't own a couch to put potatoes on (a joke), I write poems, practice affection, give great massages, ride the shopping cart in the Costco parking lot, tease, and help little old ladies across the street; you will never meet a nicer man or a badder boy.

I am a man's man, a gentleman, fit, tall, very active. I enjoy cultural, family and outdoor activities: the ballet, symphony, opera in the park, local theater, expressive dance, concerts, museums; art galleries; tasting fine food, ale and wine. I love gardens/flowers, beaches, hiking, whitewater-ocean and flat-water kayaking and rafting; Traveling is fun - day trips and far away: Canada, Mendocino, Carmel, Washington, DC, San Diego, the Sierras or Siskiyou (all recently); Locally I enjoy movies, eating family meals, running, swimming, reading (Lincoln's memoirs, book of famous quotes, Carly

Fiorina's book and lots of technical papers), the company of friends and family and downtime/vegging-type rest.

I am not just an optimist; I am the kind of positive individual who believes the glass will never be empty. Not because the contents won't go away but because I have the freedom, power and ability to keep it full, and if the original brew is no longer available, I can find another to fill the glass.

What I am looking for:

I want to meet a woman who is over her past hurts, fully available for love and adventure, smart (both street and book), resourceful, active, positive, progressive, and experimental, who enjoys most of the activities I enjoy and has a bad girl in her sweet heart.

I'd like to find a relationship that allows me to support my mate (most women are looking for a very traditional relationship -- I am not), one that is nontraditional -- unusual, growing, interesting and extraordinary. Where the two of us together are better than the sum of ourselves and we can toss out gender roles and concentrate on more important things.

I have a servant in me that I use all the time for work and my kids. I'd like to find a woman who would really get enjoyment out of being served and being empowered as a leader. I am looking for a woman who wants that very much -- with passion.

Who I am looking for:

You'd be 5'8" or taller, physically fit, 35-55 years old (with the right person, age, height and weight are almost irrelevant). You'd see yourself as a natural leader and bright. You likely scared many guys off with your personality. You'd enjoy a guy who is supportive of your independence, assertiveness/aggression, and experimentation. You'd be active but not always doing things. You'd see yourself as capable and talented, and want a mate who empowers you to do greater things. You'd likely have some kinks, desires and passions and want a partner supportive of those. I imagine you are actively looking and often surf the ads of guys instead of waiting until they find you.

Must have (I did not publish this)

- 35-55 born female
- Fit: keeps active
- Outdoor activities: rafting, swimming, hiking, camping, gardens
- Indoor activities: ballet, dining, theater, dance, art
- Pretty face
- Nice voice
- Intellectual or intelligent
- Educated (Bachelor's or better)
- Cannot be submissive by nature
- Successful in her own right
- Positive-minded

Want to have

- Kayaking and rafting
- Motorcycle rides

Nice to have

- Tech industry
- Christian
- Liberal politically
- C cup

A little prose that I used to break the ice:

Morning in the mist

-mist-covered land exposes only what it will
-faint shadows familiar images shrouded
-occasional ducks laughing
          telling jokes to their friends
-city silenced by voices in mist from chatty birds
-most never hear the mist speak,
          never smell the dank
-just early morning joggers,
          visitors from the east, a few like me
-most never venture out past rest in their beds
-missing all the best of it
-never feeling the peace
          of morning's cool air on skin
-they can only imagine the swoosh of black birds passing overhead
-dream of watching swallows
          cart wheel caching their breakfast in beak
-missing egrets barking in the flapping of wings
-I will miss this morning
-never seeing one like it again

A sample of my canned response:

"Both of us know from experience how difficult it is to make things work, so I have taken a new strategy to look for someone like myself in many ways. I reasoned that if I like me, then I would also like someone like me. Trouble is, I am a rare bird. The reason we are available is that the relationships we had 'ended,' or, more positively, 'transitioned to something else.'

"I am a complex person; I have in me a wild side, a very conservative person, a genteel man, and a guy who allows his mind to wander where it will. I don't think of these as dichotomies but rather benefits to being me. Benefits I share.
It is a deal I made with myself in my late 30s to embrace all of me. It was not until then that I truly liked myself as a person. I like who I have become, reconciling all of me, and I want to enjoy life with a woman I love for a very long time. Falling in love is such fun -- I wish it could last forever.

"I am 6'4", medium build, light brown hair, and fair-skinned -- but that does not accurately describe me, just as 5'8" tall, trim, light brown hair, and fair-skinned does not accurately describe you. We are more complex than that.

"I read ads and see common threads: most everyone wants fun, laughing, honesty, so the ads read "come dance with me," "where is my prince," "are there any good men left." Emotionally, everyone wants their basic needs met, but most do not discuss what they really want so they are not likely to find it, myself included. So I figured if I found someone like me, then we would be able to share at a much deeper level the things that are really important aside from the basic things everyone seems to want.

"I tend to be gentle but have an aggressive side too. I am one of those rare people with discretion who keeps your confidential information between us.

"One thing in your profile that caught my eye was your use of…"

(This strategy was not without its ups and downs, but overall the quality of the women I began to meet improved.)

Chapter Thirty

eHarmonizing

One website in particular, eHarmony.com, gave me the best results for personality matching, but not good matches for the different walks of life. You know, how well you fit together in how you spend your time, what career choices you made or where you like to vacation or play. So even though I'd be matched with five candidates a day, most would not work out.

I rejected all who did not meet my physical criteria and then applied the rest of my list to the process the website provided for getting to know someone. eHarmony matched me with a deputy sheriff, a substance abuse counselor, a secretary, a nurse's assistant and a chief financial officer in a single day -- now, that is variety. I imagine I went through 50 profiles to actually meet five women, which is better statistically than the other sites I frequented. I met five women this way but no sparks flew.

None provided
Age: 40
Height: 5' 6"
Body Type: Slender
Hair Color: Black

techeeandmore
None Provided

Occupation: Programmer

Matches My Love Settings	....	✧✧✧✧
Matches My Distance Settings	....	✧✧✧
Did She Match Her Profile	....	✧✧✧✧✧
Did She Match Her Photos	....	✧✧✧✧✧
Did We Have Fun	....	✧
Impression of Her as a Person	....	✧✧✧✧✧

"Nice woman, kind of shy"

What attracted me: Her rapid responses to my questions.

The first eHarmonizer was a software professional; she and I were hot after responding to each other's questions, and she was cute. The flurry of emails and IMs was almost frightening; here was a woman who could keep up with me and presumably was hungry for a relationship! We met at Tully's, but as we drank coffee we sank with the realization that we were just not well suited. She was quiet, I am not; she was shy, I am not. Strike!

Next was a nurse who had only provided pictures of herself from the waist up and all in her scrubs. I almost passed, but she sent me a provocative note and asked about sex. Now there is a subject I am interested in! We took our emails off eHarmony to the safety of our personal mail and had an interesting exchange about sex. The day of our coffee date, she confessed to being wide in the hips and was trying to lose weight. I should have just cashed out there, but we met anyway. Starbucks was crowded, so we got our coffee and sat outside. She wore a long coat and when she unbuttoned it so she could sit, it revealed a lower half three times the size of the upper. It was nighttime and she was my neighbor, so I talked with her for about an hour and we pleasantly parted company.

This was the weakness at eHarmony, I thought. They did the personality thing very well, but when it came to physical attributes and chemistry, they were less successful.

Afterthoughts: *"It was awkward meeting someone when I did not have anything to say. I felt disingenuous even staying for coffee – sometimes it just does not work out."*

None provided
Age: 47
Height: 5' 8"
Body Type: Few extra pounds
Hair Color: Brown

seemyresume
None Provided

Occupation: Recruiter

Matches My Love Settings	....	☆☆☆☆☆
Matches My Distance Settings	....	☆☆☆☆
Did She Match Her Profile	....	☆☆☆☆☆
Did She Match Her Photos	....	☆☆☆
Did We Have Fun	....	☆☆☆☆☆
Impression of Her as a Person	....	☆☆☆☆☆

"Nice woman – great catch for someone"

What attracted me: Her rapid responses to my questions.

Nina was a human resources recruiter for a consulting company; she was one of those women you'd trust with your kids the minute you knew her. We arranged a date at a Starbucks and then had dinner. She was not a dreamy looker but had lots to talk about and was truly interested in me and in making conversation to keep me interested. Our date ended with a steamy kiss in the parking lot. I did note the word "submissive" in one of our conversations, so I asked about it in an email, and she categorically said she was interested in being submissive sexually.

Nina invited me for dinner at her place on the water on the Peninsula. I arrived with flowers and wine, which impressed her. We took a walk before dinner along the waterfront near her home. She was a singer in a band for fun, and described her passion for it as we walked along energetically.

Before dinner I held her and told her how much I appreciated her cooking for me. Then I looked more closely and realized she was heating up stuff from Trader Joes. Oh, well, it tasted good. Before we ate, I got a passionate kiss. After dinner she played a few songs for me as we sat on the couch finishing the bottle of wine. After she put away her guitar I asked her directly about surrender. She blushed and admitted enjoying that. It was already 10 p.m. by then and I needed to make a decision as we made out on the couch. She put my hands on her in places I welcomed, but I was looking for something else, so I made my exit, kissing passionately all the way out the door. Nina and I still keep in touch.

None provided
Age: 40
Height: 5' 9"
Body Type: Few extra
pounds
Hair Color: Brown

veryverysweet
None Provided

Occupation: Business Owner

Matches My Love Settings	....	☼☼☼☼☼
Matches My Distance Settings	....	☼☼☼
Did She Match Her Profile	....	☼☼☼☼☼
Did She Match Her Photos	....	☼☼☼☼☼
Did We Have Fun	....	☼
Impression of Her as a Person	....	☼

"Wondered if she worked for the CIA"

What attracted me: Her rapid responses to my questions.

Helen was a beauty who owned a pastry business in a nearby town. Our coffee date lasted less than 10 minutes, as she was called away on an emergency. I always wondered if that was an escape play. Why would someone need to escape from a coffee date?

None provided
Age: 38
Height: 5' 6"
Body Type: Average
Hair Color: Brown

brendaandme
None Provided

Occupation: Business Owner

Matches My Love Settings	....	☆☆☆☆☆
Matches My Distance Settings	....	☆☆☆
Did She Match Her Profile	....	☆☆☆☆☆
Did She Match Her Photos	....	☆☆☆☆
Did We Have Fun	....	☆☆
Impression of Her as a Person	....	☆☆☆

"Hard to read"

What attracted me: Her responses to my questions.

For those who love animals, Brenda was the woman for you. She was a professional woman who loved all kinds of animals. We met near her home in the early evening and shared some conversation over mocha frappuchinos.

Then I started having flashbacks from my marriage. My ex was the owner if dozens of animals. I remember the piles of rabbit droppings, and a bird that destroyed door moldings, the drama of burying a horse, escaped snakes and then there were the spiders, creepy!

"Squawk!" I swear I heard a squawk and turned around to look. I don't know if I was sweating when I left, but I think so. My nerves were shot; I was thinking about getting home to my quiet, non-animal apartment, I drove way over the speed limit getting there. I think because Brenda's love for animals reminded me of my ex so much, it kept me from ever contacting her again.

Damn, I thought as I drove home, personality matching must not be an exact science. I reasoned that people project who they think they want to be, how they what to be seen, and Lord knows we don't always have a clear perspective on how others see us.

None provided
Age: 45
Height: 5' 9"
Body Type: Average
Hair Color: Brown

freethegerbals
None Provided

Occupation: Business Owner

Matches My Love Settings	....	☼☼☼☼☼
Matches My Distance Settings	....	☼☼☼
Did She Match Her Profile	....	☼☼
Did She Match Her Photos	....	☼☼☼☼
Did We Have Fun	....	☼
Impression of Her as a Person	....	☼

"Oh my God – not in this lifetime"

What attracted me: Her rapid responses to my questions.

A woman from Berkeley was next. She said she was an architect but when I asked about projects, all she talked about was social consciousness. She said she was a Ph.D., but I doubted that. We met on College Avenue at a local and quite famous coffee dive on a very cold morning. That woman could not stop talking. She was lit up about injustice, unfairness, men who lie, cruelty to animals, and the plight of immigrants. She never took a breath and talked even when she drank her tea. "Another tea drinker," I thought. I got up and excluded myself to leave and she kept on talking. I wondered if she even heard me, so I said, "Did you hear me, I need to go now, I have some work to do today." She talked through that and finally said "I don't think we are suited for each other." I laughed so hard out loud, I could have peed my pants. I just walked away laughing.

WHAT'S IN A WORD ANYWAY?

None provided
Age: 49
Height: 5' 10"
Body Type: Few extra pounds
Hair Color: Brown

rebeccaann12
None Provided

Occupation: Executive

Matches My Love Settings	....	☆☆☆☆☆
Matches My Distance Settings	....	☆☆☆
Did She Match Her Profile	....	☆☆☆☆☆
Did She Match Her Photos	....	☆
Did We Have Fun	....	☆☆☆☆☆
Impression of Her as a Person	....	☆☆☆☆☆

"Sweet"

What attracted me: Her rapid responses to my questions, long virtual relationship and we connected in many ways before meeting.

Despite being a bit heavy, Rebecca was a great catch. We shared a lot in common and had the same life interests. Rebecca was an executive with a finance company and next in line to run the place. I was traveling so it took a bit more time than usual to actually meet. When we finally did, it was awkward. Over the long period we had shared so much of ourselves and our intimate thoughts that when we actually met, it was sort of like kissing my sister.

Chapter Thirty-One

The five negotiable food groups

About this time it finally all started coming together for me: I was focused on meeting the type of woman who was interested in me and I in them, period. It was becoming more of a science than an art. The artful side was the chemistry; not the search or the personality fit.

The kind of woman I wanted was independent, active, had a brain and used it, felt good about her ideas and was willing to try new things. I found these woman after a few emails by offering some ideas about relationships that either they agreed with or were willing to learn more about. For my own, personal organizational purposes in this strategy, I called them life's "food groups."

My idea was that no one should or could be anyone other than who they were at their very core. That is why my marriage failed; I could not be myself because she did not want me to be me, but someone she *wanted* me to be. My core personality was not a benefit to her and hers most definitely was not for me. That's why I was looking for someone who benefited simply from me being myself!

I mean, what a simple, yet unique realization! Why had no one come up with this before? Out of all the techniques I'd read about regarding "How to catch and keep a woman" and so on, and after all this time seeking the right person – the soul mate – I had never really considered the nexus of what this all meant – that in order for people to be truly happy together, they have to be able to learn something, or benefit, from the other person.

It just suddenly made crystal-clear sense to me, and because of that core inside of each of us, I reasoned that men and women could successfully negotiate a strong relationship.

I thought about just what couples want or need to negotiate -- things like fidelity, exclusivity, life direction, sexual activity, hobbies and other things people do for fun, and other ideas occurred to me as likely things to be negotiated. Again, no one talks about these openly – I wonder why not?

After several months of thinking and having practice conversations with the women I was encountering, I was beginning to solidify my ideas. You cannot negotiate chemistry or love. No one can trade their core personality with any level of success, no matter how "moldable" they might be, and you just cannot tell who might be able and willing to consider discussing these kinds of things.

I learned by trial and error that women who think in terms of "destiny" don't want to discuss these issues because that is not how destiny works, at least in their minds. Women who are shy and cautious do not want to discuss them because it quickly exposes their true needs and it makes them insecure and vulnerable. So, the only women who were willing to discuss them were the type of women I was looking for – yippee! Finally, a light bulb went on, and it wasn't 35 watts, either!

Here's how I designed my "food groups":

1). How you spend your time.
2). Sex.
3). Money (how it is spent).
4). Life direction.
5). Household and life chores.

All of these things can be negotiated. So getting some of these items answered up front seemed like a good idea while considering a long-term relationship with a woman.

- ***Why these factors helped me meet the right kind of woman***: Without a clear understanding between both people, the relationship will, without a single doubt, fail. There are lots of kinds of women and personality traits, habits and activities that dictate how well couples will get along. You have to ask these questions both of yourself and your potential mate: How much personal space do I need? Who will do the dishes? How will we decide when and on what money is spent? Those kinds of questions must be dealt with in every relationship, and often, they carry unspoken expectations. So if they are not discussed, they are just assumed. There lies the crux of all the troubles and drama of relationships -- conflict from unspoken expectations. The "he thought she would, and she thought he would" kind of dialogue. Who the hell is responsible for the dishes anyway? You'd think reasonable people wouldn't make an issue out of such a small thing; the dishes are dirty, so clean them up! Easy! But when the expectations lie there, it becomes a big deal. So it's important to get the expectations out in the open because even if I don't care about the dishes thing, she might.

Also, knowing this gave me the ability to filter out nine out of every 10 women I encountered and allowed me to fine-tune my coffee dates to women who were closer to my ideal mate. If only I could then find one in 10 during coffee dates, I would have a winner of a formula and I would meet the kind of woman who would appreciate me and benefit from who I am as a person without changing me at my core.

- ***How I could tell the women were right for me***: Being able to discuss the food groups gave me the advantage I was looking for. I could meet independent woman and have a very rational conversation with them that, in theory, they too would be eager to have. Women who resisted the conversation were not thinking about relationships in the same light that I was, which I recognized immediately and thus saved time for both of us. They held some combination of ideas that stopped them from connecting with me. Women who were not ready to consider a long-term relationship did not want to engage in that type of conversation. Women who were afraid of the risk of exposing what they truly wanted shied away. "Destined-oriented" women tired of the conversation quickly because they wanted a relationship "to just be the way God meant it to be."

Chapter Thirty-Two

One more "Miss adventure"

Frighteningly, I was beginning to like the misadventures more than the good dates because they gave me more material to think and write about. There was something to be said for oddities and alternate lifestyles. Just meeting a woman for coffee was not very interesting compared to slaves and romance.

As I drank my morning coffee and read my email every day, I began to wonder if I was unconsciously seeking that alternative sort of relationship; I knew I was certainly getting very good at spotting them and I did rather respond to them more often than someone less attractive, and Thelma was not an exception.

Real life is better then fiction
Age: 49
Height: 5' 8"
Body Type: Slender
Hair Color: Blond

seizethedays

I'd love to meet a man who turns my mind and body on. A man with confidence, a little arrogance, moxie and an inner peace that shows on the outside.

Occupation: Sales Executive

Matches My Love Settings	....	☆☆☆☆☆
Matches My Distance Settings	....	☆☆☆
Did She Match Her Profile	....	☆☆☆☆☆
Did She Match Her Photos	....	☆☆☆☆
Did We Have Fun	....	☆☆☆
Impression of Her as a Person	....	☆☆☆

"Strange days have found us"

What attracted me: Her photos and the language in her ad.

Thelma was a sales consultant for a large software firm. She traveled frequently, and as a benefit of this travel made side trips to photograph the people of Third-World countries. She was fascinated with the faces of suffering people and with the dilemmas they faced. I was winding down my campaign and almost ready to give up because the effort was exhausting, even to a type A like me.

Thelma contacted me from Match.com. I did the basic once-over and noticed that her photos were quite different from others; they showed her in various troubled areas of the world as well as at parties and in her bikini.

She was attracted by the wording in my ad and asked me a simple question: "Do you enjoy traveling to meet people from other cultures?"

Truthfully, I had not done that and told her so, but I also told her that I was fascinated with cultures -- just not of the modern kind. I told her of my interest in language acquisition, root word meaning, linguistics, and the history of human relationships. We did the food group conversation via email, and she was very down to earth about each one. We carried on like that for a few weeks, and then she asked to meet. I like assertive women, so I said a resounding "when?" She was level-headed, interesting, extremely intelligent and gifted – a nice package deal.

Thelma was doing a show of her photos at a studio in San Jose, so we met near the show and had coffee. She was a slender woman with bright eyes and a thin face. Not a looker like some I'd seen, but a woman of some substance and obviously captivated by the intellectual and visual aspects of life. We talked about her travels and I found myself listening to a well-spoken woman with genuine concern for the plight of people. She intentionally went into war-torn areas and took photos. Whoa, that was way outside my comfort zone.

One good thing about Thelma was that she loved to hike and looked pretty good in shorts and boots, so we make a trip to Castle Rock and hiked around the place. It was late in the year and many of the trees had turned or lost their leaves, so the place with quite different than my hikes there before. She took pictures from time to time and we talked about the colors and contrasts of gray and brown we encountered along the way.

At the exact rock where I picnicked with another woman, she pressed me back against the cliff side and we had our first kiss and more as she reached under my shirt. I slowly sat down against the rock and she lowered herself with me as I reciprocated. I thought we were going to do it right there, as we got pretty worked up. Then she slowed her pace and said, "We do have chemistry, don't we?" She was sitting on my lap, and I began again, but she moved away as if something calling her had taken her attention. She turned around and sat against me, panting a bit, and looking at the scenery. She had gone into her mind somewhere far away.

Castle Rock is a tough hike, and we got to the end in that inevitable sweaty state, where we once again kissed, pressing against each other. As we drove back to her car I asked her to lunch at a funky Saratoga place I had been to several times. She agreed, and as we ate, I suggested we see a play. She said, "No, I don't think so." I suggested a trip to Carmel, and again she said, "It's not really my thing." So I asked her where she would like to go, and she said she wanted to watch people in some place where things are real. I choked on that for a minute because the thought of a date not being real unless it was done in the shadow of despair or of poverty had a distasteful feel to it. Id bet those people in that place she wanted to go wanted to dressed up, wanted to go on dates, to plays, and probably even would like to see Carmel – did life really have to have so much despair?

We kissed as we parted, but we never made a plan for another date. I postulated that she was either a well-to-do woman who felt guilt for her prosperity or a woman who felt better while being involved with someone else's troubles. Neither felt good to me, so I never returned her email.

About the time Thelma faded away and Teresa and I had dried up I met her, a woman I would spend the next 18 extraordinary months with. Finally, there she was, coffee date #33, but that is another story.

Afterthoughts: *"I told Thelma I wanted to retire in Africa. I think that is what hit off our connection. It was a mistake to think of retirement as an adventure, I guess, but I just wanted to work with orphans who need a father figure, not to be a voyeur to poverty"*

Chapter Thirty-Three

Adding up all the hype

Buy the time I met Vicky, my very special #33, I had been "coffee_and_conversation," "fremonttechguy," "freealertalive," and "youndalertalive." The experience was both wonderful and maddening, but meeting Vicky finally put it all together for me.

This journey was a maturing process for me as a man. All my preconceived notions of women, relationships and love were severely tested and because of it, I was a changed man.

Each of my strategies in attracting women tested what I believed about myself and who I was looking for. I found that the truth about me is deep inside, and that under all the complications lives a simple guy with a simple faith -- a faith in soul mates and a faith in true love.

 I am still a believer, even after all that.

TAKING A BREAK FROM DATING

Epilogue

If ever I had a hope for me
If ever I had for you
I'd hope for love and transparency
I'd hope for love to come true

Fear not good man
Don't fret fair maid
There is only what you make of it
Only what you bring with you

Make yourself known
Free yourself

Afterthoughts: *Do I have some advice for would-be daters online? Yes; plan, adjust, and test what you think you want and who you are looking for -- it is all about asking the right questions."*

Help Me with Relationships Series

Author M. Lyman Hill is creating a series of books to help women and men with their relationships and internet dating experiences.

- **Why Do I Keep Picking The Wrong Guy?**
  - Internet dating help for women who pick the wrong men over and over again. First in this series.
- **How Can I Attract The Right Guy For Me?**
  - More Internet dating help for women who pick the wrong men over and over again. Second in this series.
- **How Can I Attract The Right Guy For Me?**
  - Internet dating help for women who pick the wrong men over and over again. The final books in this series of three.
- **Help Me Find My Soul Mate**
  - Internet dating help for women and men in finding what really matters in relationships.
- **The 5 Food Groups** - Negotiating In Relationships
  - Relationship help for couples and those looking for better relationships.
- **Help Me Find A Relationship Model That Works For Me**
  - A fresh perspective on what makes good relationships in the information age.
- **Help Me Save My Relationship**
  - A quick help guide for women who want to save their relationship.
- **Why Men Become Lazy Lovers** (what to do about it)
  - Relationship help for women

The **5** Food Groups
Negotiating In Relationships

Relationship and internet dating help for everyone who
wants a better cleaner faster relationship

One hour of your
time reading
this book will
enlighten you

By M. Lyman Hill
author of My First 32 Coffee Dates

Available spring 2011